Levitation

Steve Richards

What It Is, How It Works,
How to Do It

CORONET

This edition first published in Great Britain in 2015 by Coronet
An imprint of Hodder & Stoughton
An Hachette UK company

1

A CIP catalogue record for this title is available from the British Library

ISBN 978 1 473 60639 5
Ebook ISBN 978 1 473 60638 8

Printed and bound by CPI Group (UK) Ltd, Croydon, CR0 4YY

Hodder & Stoughton policy is to use papers that are natural, renewable and
recyclable products and made from wood grown in sustainable forests.
The logging and manufacturing processes are expected to conform
to the environmental regulations of the country of origin.

Hodder & Stoughton Ltd
Carmelite House
50 Victoria Embankment
London EC4Y 0DZ

www.hodder.co.uk

CONTENTS

Acknowledgements   iv

1. Can Man Fly?   1

2. The Gravity of It All   11

3. Fakirs and Fakers   23

4. A Word with You   45

5. Astral Energies   59

6. Some Practical Secrets   69

7. The Element of Will   85

8. Sanyama   99

9. So You Can Fly . . . Now What?   125

Appendix   139

Notes   143

Index   153

ACKNOWLEDGMENTS

I would like to thank Mr. Stephen Rozman of Tougaloo College for his very interesting interview; the editors of The Theosophical Publishing House in Madras, India, for permission to quote some early articles from *The Theosophist*; Mr. Don Barcell of Campbell, California, for the loan of his photograph and permission to reproduce it; the staff of the Sivananda Yoga Vedanta Centres, International, for the photographs and information they provided, as well as for permission to reproduce their photographs; and finally the staff of the Olcott Library and Research Centre in Wheaton, Illinois, for their assistance in locating articles and loaning documents.

CHAPTER ONE

CAN MAN FLY?

Levitation! Is it for real? Students of psychic phenomena have been asking that question for centuries, and not getting many answers. Levitation is a rather unique kind of psychic phenomenon. It is not like astral projection, or psychometry, or precognition. It is the sort of thing Joseph of Cupertino might have done three centuries ago, or that some *mahatma* in India or Tibet might do today. But it is not the kind of thing an ordinary person would expect to do. And certainly not in the Western World.

That is why a lot of eyebrows were raised in mid-1977 when the Maharishi Mahesh Yogi announced that not only could *he* levitate; he could teach *others* to do it, too. After all, the Maharishi Mahesh Yogi is famous for his Transcendental Meditation (TM) technique. He has a reputation for methods that are not only simple to teach and easy to learn, but also that work – and work well.

'Levitation is the most profound of the siddhis yet available,' a TM instructor told me. 'Maharishi says it's all a matter of mind-body coordination. Tell your body to walk and it does it. No problem. But tell it to rise into the air "by mere intention" and it doesn't. Improve your mind-body coordination and you can do that too.'

It all sounded familiar. Since the early seventies TM people have been amassing study after study, showing that meditators have better memories than other people, sleep better, run faster, make better grades in school, even see better. One TM instructor I interviewed even says meditators have fewer cavities. But levitation?

'It's not so strange,' was the reply. 'In the Vedas, which are the oldest records of human achievement, there are stories of people doing these things. These abilities were heretofore considered to be "supernatural," but they are now being found to be within the range of normal human potential.

'The emphasis of the programme is not an isolated demonstration of powers, but rather an accelerated growth towards the state of Enlightenment through the development of special abilities which enliven consciousness in the field of all possibilities.'

I was told that the programme is called the TM-Sidhi Programme, 'sidhi' being the preferred TM spelling of the Sanskrit word *siddhi*, which means 'accomplishment,' or occult powers. There are Eight Great Siddhis in the yogic tradition, from which TM is ultimately derived, and probably even more in the Sidhi Programme. Levitation is only one of them.

'You mustn't think in terms of flying for long distances,' I was told. 'Our people are flying only a few feet at a time now. It's a progressive development. Take, for example, the siddhi of unlimited strength. The first time you do the siddhi you may feel only a slight sensation. But each time you do it you get stronger and stronger, until finally you do have unlimited strength.

'Maharishi says that there are sixty-four channels of Enlightenment in the human body through which the siddhis manifest themselves. You perform certain exercises and the siddhis emerge from out of the Absolute.

'There are about seventy of these siddhis in all, but we don't practise all of them. Maharishi has found some of them to be more beneficial than others.'

Among those Maharishi has found to be more beneficial are Strength, Friendliness, Omniscience, and Invisibility, as well as Levitation. There are rumours that some meditators are even walking through walls.

Maharishi mentioned the siddhis as early as 1962, when he wrote *The Science of Being and Art of Living*. But in the early years of the TM movement there was too much to do just promoting the idea of meditation and the basic TM technique to worry much about powers. The channels of communication were kept open, though, and advanced meditators were encouraged to tell of their experiences at teacher training courses.

They had plenty to tell. Some felt that they had become invisible or that they could see through other people. Still others had visions of spiritual beings. One instructor, now out of the movement, recalls:

'I frequently experienced the sensation of becoming gaseous, first filling the room, then expanding over the Mediterranean Sea (while in Spain), and finally extending throughout the universe.'[1]

These experiences are of course known to Western scientists. In *The Relaxation Response*, Dr. Benson of Harvard University says that 'from our personal observations, many people who meditate for several hours every day for weeks at a time tend to hallucinate.'[2] But these scientists tend to write the experience off. The theory is that meditation causes sensory deprivation, and that in turn causes the brain to create its own excitement in the form of 'siddhi' experiences.

There is not much doubt, though, that the siddhis experienced by advanced TM meditators are the very same siddhis described in ancient yogic texts. And that raises a serious question. If the siddhis are not real – if they are in fact mere symptoms of sensory deprivation – an important part of the yogic tradition is called into question.

As a yogi, and a yogi who had access to large numbers of devoted siddhi-experience experiencers, Maharishi felt the need to determine the truth. He purchased two old hotels in Seelisberg, a little town in Switzerland overlooking Lake Lucerne, and founded the Maharishi European Research University (MERU).

The hotels were the Kulm and the Sonnenberg. They were restored at a cost of about two million pounds and painted in TM's favourite colours: cream and yellow. Finally, in April 1975, MERU was dedicated.

At first, the rooms were rented out to advanced meditators who wanted to meditate for extended periods in a semi-monastic environment. But in 1976 Maharishi started investigating the siddhis themselves.

He started out with just a few people who had been meditating for an extraordinarily long time – fifteen or twenty years. Basing himself on the *Yoga Sutras* of Patanjali, Maharishi worked out simple exercises, or 'formulas', to encourage the siddhis to manifest themselves. The first siddhas were not told what to expect, and some of them were startled when they found out. As one of them put it:

'Everything happened so fast that before I knew it, I was breaking boundaries that I had never experienced before in my life.'[3]

Subjective siddhis, such as the ability to see hidden things and techniques for 'refining intuition', were included. But the emphasis was on objective siddhis – things that could be noted – especially levitation and invisibility. There is hardly any way a person can hallucinate himself into the air. He either levitates or he does not. And if he does, that proves that something significant is happening. It also proves that the person has reached a certain state of what TM people call 'Enlightenment'. A person who rises three feet into the air is said to be more enlightened than a person who only rises two. And a person who can levitate a foot in the air is more enlightened than a person who cannot levitate at all.

The first small group of siddhas was asked to help train others, and so it went. All throughout 1976 siddhi instruction was given to advanced meditators. When the students graduated, they were dubbed 'executive governors of consciousness' because they had acquired the ability to 'govern the trend of time.'

In December, nine hundred TM instructors from all over the world converged on the Seelisberg campus for six months of intensive instruction in the siddhis. According to one of their number, 40 per cent of them levitated, and a few even disappeared.[4] All of those who disappeared reappeared eventually, we trust, and in May of the following year the class graduated.

Until then, the course had been called the 'Governor Training Course of the Age of Enlightenment' and had been open to teachers only. Stage magician Doug Henning was the only non-instructor allowed to take the course.[5] But starting in May, a new and simplified version of the course was offered to the public – the TM-Sidhi Programme. The new siddhas were organised into promotional teams and sent into the world. Thirty of these teams were sent to the United States alone.[6]

The TM-Sidhi course was offered in two stages: Phase I and Phase II. Phase I was conceived as a 'preparatory' programme – four to eight weeks spent at a 'Capital of the Age of Enlightenment' in order to 'stabilise pure awareness.'[7] Phase II included actual instruction in the siddhis themselves and was organised into four two-week blocks, all to be taken in residence.

I was able to find out about the content of Phase I from one of TM's dissatisfied customers. Mr. Stephen Rozman is chairman of the Department of Political Science at Tougaloo College in Tougaloo, Mississippi. He was also one of the very first enrollees in the prep course when it was first offered in the United States. I asked him what the course consisted of.

'Just a lot of long hours of meditation,' he said. 'We didn't get any new techniques except for a pranayama technique. And the instructors did lecture, but it was nothing startling.'

'What most troubled me at the prep course was the constant change in the programme and the waiting until the last moment to tell us that levitation was an "advanced siddhi" which would demand fifteen hundred extra dollars and four more weeks of time.'

'I don't want to come down too hard on them because it seems to me sometimes that I don't see the whole picture. People who have been through the courses at later dates and other sites have told me that their experiences were more positive.'

Mr. Rozman did not stay for the siddhi programme itself, because he had enrolled initially with the understanding that he would receive levitation instructions within six weeks.

Phase I was later phased out. Then the requirement that potential siddhas had to be meditators for six months was relaxed. Now a meditator is eligible for the siddhi course three months after he learns how to meditate. After that, Phase II was replaced temporarily with a forty day 'accelerated' programme, all in an effort to make it easier for people to take the courses. Finally, a part-time siddhi programme was worked out, which requires attendance at a TM centre for two nights a week for six weeks, followed by two weeks in residence to learn the 'flying siddhi' – levitation. 'Maharishi's making this available to *everybody*,' an instructor told me.

The irony of it is, though, that Maharishi is *not* making it available to everybody. The greatest single deterrent to would-be siddhas is not the time required to take the course but the price. And the price has yet to come down.

The prices seem to vary from one country to another. In the United States, Phase I, when it was being offered, cost $245 per week, which brought the total price of the prep programme alone to from $980 to $1,960, depending on whether you were required to stay for four weeks or eight weeks. That is $35 per day, and includes room and board as well as whatever instruction is offered. Not much more than one would expect to pay for a good hotel room, but a hefty sum none the less.

After Phase I came Phase II, at slightly higher prices. The entire Phase II programme costs, at the time of writing, $3,000, or $750 per two-week block. If you take the programme in residence you are allowed to pay for it $750 at a time, at the beginning of each block. But if you take the part-time six-week version, you are required to pay the entire $3,000 at once in advance.

In Canada the prices are somewhat higher. Mr. Bob Pepper is quoted by the *Vancouver Sun* as saying that the prep course alone would cost 'a minimum of $3,430' Canadian.[8] In Britain,

Michael Hellicar of the *Daily Mirror* quotes a price of something over a thousand pounds.[9] The prices are all roughly comparable if one considers the exchange rates and the differences in wages and living costs from one country to the next.

Even at those rates, I am told that twenty thousand people have signed up for the siddhi courses since they were first offered in 1977. That is a lot less than the two million or so who have taken the basic course. But in purely financial terms, twenty thousand siddhas represents the same income to the movement as four hundred thousand meditators.

When the courses were first offered, they were promoted in a vigorous advertising campaign. Display advertisements appeared in the *Village Voice* and the *Montreal Star* promising free lectures on 'the ability to levitate by mere intention through the Transcendental Meditation Programme.' According to *Newsweek*, though, when people arrived for the free lectures, 'many were sorely disappointed and at some centres there were shouts of "put up or shut up" from the audience.' The lectures did not include any of the secrets whereby levitation was to be accomplished. And they did not include demonstrations.[10]

In an interview with the *Washington Post*, Baltimore lawyer David Sykes explained that 'we don't want to get into a circus demonstration type of environment.' But he did say that 'if a maximum of ten people, but no more, donate a minimum of $1,000 to the programme, then we'd show them.'[11] There is every reason to believe the offer was made in good faith because in a statement to the *Los Angeles Times*, printed on 29 November 1977, Mr. David Verrill repeated and clarified it.[12] According to Mr. Verrill, the ten spectators would have to pay $1,000 *each*.[13]

That is not such a high price to pay to see a man levitating, and on 16 December 1977, an attorney in Los Angeles wrote to the World Plan Executive Council in Pacific Palisades, California, to announce that the terms could be met. The money was raised by the 'Committee for the· Sincere Practice of Yoga,' which was organised by the Swami Vishnu-Devananda. The

Swami is the author of *The Complete Illustrated Book of Yoga* and *Meditation and Mantras* as well as the founder of the International Sivananda Yoga Vedanta Centres, with world headquarters in Val Morin, Quebec (Canada). He feels that as one of the world's most prominent yogis, he is the conservator of the true yogic tradition, and his attitude toward TM's levitation claims is – well, sceptical.

His scepticism may well seem justified. Despite the two offers from Mr. Sykes and Mr. Verill and his own response, not one TM instructor has yet given a public demonstration of levitation to date.* *Time* magazine intimates that a demonstration might have been forthcoming, but that word came down straight from the Maharishi's headquarters in Switzerland that such things were 'undignified.'[14]

It is worth saying, though, that there was one demonstration – at the Maharishi International University in Fairfield, Iowa, in May 1977, when the courses first came out. Four young men did the levitating, and twenty-two people were invited to watch – all but two of them meditators.

'Witnesses believed that the hopping they saw could be accomplished by experienced gymnasts,' writes reporter Aubrey Haines.

'Not so, says the directors of the National Academy of [G]ymnasts in Eugene, Oregon, who denied that skilled athletes could duplicate the feat, for "there's no means of gaining thrust with the full lotus."'[15]

Swami Vishnu would disagree with that last statement, though. He claims there is a means of gaining thrust with the full lotus. In fact, he teaches one.

What you must do is sit in the full lotus, then rock back and forth on your haunches. The first few times you do this, you will find it difficult to maintain your balance, but balance comes in

---

* Since the first publication of this book in 1980, public demonstrations of the first stage of flying have been held.

time. When it does, try to acquire momentum by rocking, and then push off from the ground at just the right moment. You will be able to 'hop' about a foot into the air.

If a photographer takes your picture with a high-speed camera, it will appear that you are suspended in the air.

This yogic technique is used to bring the energy to the brain preparatory to meditation, but it is considered to be an advanced exercise. In *Meditation and Mantras*, Swami Vishnu says that 'some spiritual groups teach the exercise to beginners. However, this is physically and psychically dangerous and is not recommended, for it causes the *prana* to move too quickly in the body. Problems can result for those who have not been practising *asanas* and more simple *pranayamas* for a number of years.'[16]

One problem can be a premature arousal of *Kundalini*, an almost mystical energy in the human system that can be extremely beneficial if aroused properly, and extremely dangerous if not. But our problem is a little different.

Swami does not say in *Meditation and Mantras* just who he means by 'some spiritual groups,' but in interviews he and his disciples have been more explicit. As I said, he is sceptical that the TM meditators are really levitating, and he suspects that the levitation photos that the TM organization has published were taken as previously described in this chapter.

Not that he is sceptical about levitation *per se*. In *Meditation and Mantras*, he says that 'these siddhis do exist,' but in a later interview with the *News World* he added certain qualifications to that statement: 'To do certain feats such as levitation takes many years of practice in breathing exercises, and diet, and no smoking or drinking or drugs.'[17]

If that is true, then obviously no one could learn to levitate in eight weeks.

But with all respect due to the Swami, and he is due a very great deal of respect, the rock-and-push 'hopping' technique is not the technique that was used for making the TM levitation photos. The Swami's photographs are ingenious, but they leave the mystery of TM levitation unsolved.

In the first place, anyone who has ever tried the Swami's hopping technique knows that a good deal of physical effort is involved. And if you look closely at his photos, you can see that the people shown 'levitating' in them are working very hard. There is a certain tension and in some cases contortion of the body that gives it away. TM meditator-levitators in the photos released by the TM organization are always shown in a relaxed position. And another point: anyone who uses Swami's methods must use his hands to push off from the ground. Otherwise he cannot rise very high. All three of the Swami's people are shown with their arms extended. That is a giveaway that would appear in any faked photo. Yet in the TM photos, the levitators usually have their hands clasped, or else they leave them drooping loosely in their laps.

There is one other thing that is not objective, but that one picks up in interviews with TM levitators and instructors, and that is their apparent sincerity. Rick Fields captured it best in his article for the *New Age* magazine. When he expressed his own doubts to New York TM instructor John Macey, Mr. Macey replied:

'But – it's – it's – I was there, and there were hundreds of people who were levitating and disappearing and just having the ability to know anything on the level of inner sense awareness – just because this pure consciousness is operating from this infinitely conscious level.'[18]

It is hard for anyone who has sensed it to set this kind of sincerity aside. It's obvious these people believe they are levitating, whether they are or not. All that remains for us is to determine whether or not their beliefs are correct.

CHAPTER TWO

THE GRAVITY OF IT ALL

What do scientists say about all this? Well, scientists say that man cannot fly, but that does not mean much. Scientists say the bumblebee cannot fly either. It seems the little creatures violate just about every known law of aerodynamics every time they leave the ground. But the bumblebee flies anyway, apparently using laws scientists do not know about. And it is possible that man can do the same.

What scientists say specifically is that a 'force' they call 'gravity' somehow holds us to the surface of the earth. Never mind what a 'force' is; scientists do not know that. And never mind what 'gravity' is; scientists do not know that, either. Scientists do know that the 'force' of 'gravity' keeps us from rising off the ground. Without gravity, levitation would not only be possible: it would be unavoidable.

So, gravitation is really the key to levitation. If the force of gravity could be somehow neutralised, or reversed, so that it pushes us away from the ground instead of holding us to it, or else be opposed by an equal and opposite force, then we would have levitation.

As Professor Perry says: 'We are so accustomed to consider gravitation as being something absolute and unalterable that the idea of a complete or partial rising in opposition to it seems inadmissible. Nevertheless, there are phenomena in which by means of material forces gravitation is overcome. In several diseases, as for instance nervous fever, the weight of the body appears to be increased, but in all ecstatic conditions to be diminished. And there may be forces other than material ones which can counteract this power.'[1]

It is a question of how gravitation works. To say that levitation is possible or impossible on the basis of scientific laws requires a knowledge of gravity's inner workings. And that is something scientists do not have.

Not that they haven't tried. According to Arthur Eddington, since Sir Isaac Newton's time there have been about two hundred theories of gravity proposed by as many theorists.[2]

One of the most popular is the gravity-is-a-field theory, which says that gravity is a field, like an electric field, or a magnetic field. If the theory is correct, gravity is a 'something' that reaches out from the surface of the earth and pulls us and everything else toward it. Some early scientists believed that the gravity field was a network of very fine threads, so fine they could not be seen with the naked eye, but which had a spring-like action on anything that was lifted from the surface of the earth. As you moved upward, these invisible springs would grow taut and pull you back down again. More recently, scientists have decided the gravity field is nonmaterial, which means they really just do not know *what* it is. But the most important implication of the gravity-is-a-field theory for us is that gravity *behaves* like a field.

In many ways, fields act like radiant energy, in that the influence they represent emanates from the surface of the field's origin and ripples through space, much like the ripples that appear on the surface of a pond when you throw a stone into it. As H. G. Wells points out in *The First Men in the Moon*:[3]

Almost all known substances are opaque to some form or other of radiant energy. Glass, for example, is transparent to light, but much less so to heat, so that it is useful as a fire-screen; and alum is transparent to light, but blocks heat completely. A solution of iodine in carbon bisulphide, on the other hand, completely blocks light but is quite transparent to heat. It will hide a fire from you but permit all its warmth to reach you. Metals are not only opaque to light and heat, but also to electrical energy, which passes through both iodine solution and glass almost as if they were not interposed.

Everything, though, is transparent to gravity, or at least everything now known. But if gravity is a field, then it makes sense that there may be a substance or an energy or something that could block the gravitational influence and make us weightless.

In *The First Men in the Moon*, Wells's character, Dr. Cavor, actually discovers such a substance and names it after himself – cavorite. Using it, he builds a spaceship and ventures for the moon. But real life scientists have been less successful.

In his book on gravity, Dr. George Gamow suggests that cavorite – if it exists – would have to have a negative mass. Now there's one for you. There is nothing mathematically absurd about negative mass, but it is difficult to imagine any real substance having it. And that, says Dr. Gamow, is the reason there are no gravity-field-shields.[4]

If a substance did have a negative mass, it would not necessarily block the gravitational influence. But gravity would repel it. Thus, instead of being drawn toward the earth, as anything with positive mass would be, our negative mass substance would be pushed away from it.

There is, in fact, a form of matter in the universe that has all the characteristics of normal matter, but in reverse. Scientists call it antimatter, and for a time it was thought that antimatter might have the requisite qualities. But in an article in *Science*, D. C. Peaslee trots out some rather imposing equations that prove (he says) that antimatter is affected by gravity in the same way as matter.[5] So the gravity-field-shields do not exist.

While I was researching this book I came across an advertisement for a booklet published by a small publishing company in California that sheds some light on this problem. The booklet is called *Frogstein's Saucer Technology*, and the author is Mr. John Bigelow of Indiana. In the advertisement, the publisher warns: 'If you can't read, have a low I.Q., or never finished high school, don't order this one,' and it is rather heavy reading. It is also rather interesting.[6]

Mr. Bigelow is the inventor of an antigravity device that he believes could potentially be used to power a spaceship. He is also the inventor of several 'No-Fuel Power' systems, which produce energy without fuel, and the publisher of 'a work of art published sporadically by Hummingbird Publications of Music and AntiGravity' – *Frogstein Papers*. He is an interesting man, and his theory about gravity shields is that gravity is a dual force. In his view, gravity operates on the astral plane as well as on the material, and constantly oscillates between these two planes of existence, whereas any material substance that might be used as a shield operates purely on the material plane. Thus, gravity can circumvent purely material energies and substance by virtue of its dual nature.

The gravity-is-a-field theory also provides for another possibility other than shielding, though. If gravity fields are polarised, as are all other kinds of fields, then the question of gravitational attraction and repulsion reduces to one of polarity.

If you take two bar magnets and put the North Pole of one close to the North Pole of the other, they repel. But if you put the North Pole of one close to the South Pole of the other, they attract. This polarity business is quite common with field phenomena, and it suggests that there might be gravitational polarities as well.

In an article in *Science Digest* Robert Forward actually describes a gravity engine based on this fact. Forward's idea is patterned after the electromagnet. To make an electromagnet, you take an iron bar and wrap coils of wire around it, then pass an electrical current through the wire. This generates a magnetic field. Now, Forward suggests that we use coils of tubing and instead of passing an electric current through the coils, he suggests that we use a very dense form of matter. This will produce a gravitational field – in theory at least – and that gravitational field will have a gravitational North and a gravitational South Pole.[7]

Depending on how we orient this artificial gravity field, it will either attract the gravitational field of the earth or it will repel it. Thus, when the engine is sitting still it will have one weight, but when we start it, its weight will either increase or decrease, depending on its position with respect to the earth.

A gravity engine of this sort could be the space propulsion system of the future, but for the moment it is a little impractical. An engine of this sort could be constructed, but the antigravity it would generate would not be enough to counteract its own weight. The engine would become lighter, but it would not leave the ground.

Now there is an alternative to the gravity-is-a-field theory, which starts out by challenging one of that theory's basic assumptions. Implicit in the gravity-is-a-field theory is the idea that gravity is also a pull. Something from the earth – we do not know what – extends from the earth's surface and pulls us toward it. There is no reason to make that assumption unless we know for a fact that the gravity field exists, which we do not. Gravity could just as easily be a push from above, and with that we come to the push-pull theory.

The push-pull theory was popular with the early mechanists – the scientists who believed that gravity was something material. In one of Sir Isaac Newton's notebooks, written in 1675, gravity is attributed to 'the pressure of a descending aetherial shower.'[8]

The ether is, of course, supposed to be a very fine form of matter, rarer than the rarest gas, which exists throughout the universe. If Newton's theory is correct, this ether is constantly showering down on us and literally blowing us toward the earth's surface. For this to be true, though, something would have to be causing this 'aetherial' shower. We would have to suppose that there is a super-ether that showers down on the ether, and that would lead to a superduperether that would shower down upon the super-ether, and so forth.

This is what philosophers call the infinite regress. It is absurd, and it is the reason why, in 1679, Newton abandoned the push-pull hypothesis for 'action at a distance.'

That was it for the push-pull hypothesis for two centuries. In the later nineteenth century push-pull was dusted off by an American named Cyrus Teed and presented in an altogether original form.

Cyrus Teed was born in Moravia, New York, in 1839 and started out to be a doctor of the 'eclectic' medical system. Studying in the Eclectic Medical College in New York City, Teed acquired something of a scientific education that he put to use in independent experimentation. In 1869 he proved – to his own satisfaction – 'that the universe is all one substance, limited, balanced, integral, and emanating from one source.'[9] There were religious overtones in all this – the 'one source' was supposed to be God – and it is therefore not surprising that Teed eventually traded in his medical bag for a pulpit. He was not slow in having a vision in which he was appointed the earthly representative of Jesus Christ, and shortly thereafter he founded what was to become the 'Koreshan Unity' – his very own religious utopian community.

Teed combined Fundamentalism with the occult and his own rather unorthodox scientific theories. He taught reincarnation, alchemy, and communism, as well as the 'Cellular Cosmogony,' which became a book in 1898.

The Cellular Cosmogony grew out of Teed's idea that the universe must necessarily be finite. Most astronomers believed that the universe was infinite, but Teed believed that it must have definite boundaries. That is not such an unreasonable view, and Einstein promoted a similar theory many years later, but Einstein might not have agreed with Teed's interpretation of it.

In the Cellular Cosmogony, the universe is the earth, a sphere 8,000 miles in diameter. Instead of living on the outside of the earth, we live on the inside, for which reason Teed's theory has been called the 'outside-in' theory. The sun is just a reflection of something else – an idea that Madame Blavatsky took up at one time – and the stars are reflections from seven mercurial discs that float in the earth's centre. The earth's shell has seventeen layers, and so on, and so on, and so on.

It is quite a complicated theory, and not entirely unscientific, since it is based on a series of experiments Teed conducted with his friend U. G. Morrow in 1896 and 1897. But the main point of interest for us is what Teed thought about gravity.

'Gravity really descends from above,' he wrote, 'consequently, it has a tendency to push objects instead of pulling them. Light and heat are forms of gravic energy. That which is called gravity is but one of ten thousand qualities of descending gravic energy. Gravic energies are cathode; consequently they descend. Levic energies are anode; hence, they ascend.'[10]

Before man first ventured into space, the outside-in-theory was not at all easy to disprove. It ran against the grain of orthodox scientific thinking, but in the same way as Copernicus' heliocentric theory did three centuries before. And Teed's theories impressed some influential people, among them a former member of the Royal Astronomical Society.

Just after World War II, the theory also appears to have impressed an amateur astronomer from the Argentine, Mr. Antonio Duran Navarro, who gave it an interesting twist.

Mr. Navarro accepts most of Teed's ideas – we live on the inside of a spherical earth, the earth is 8,000 miles in diameter – but he insists that gravity is centrifugal force, not a 'levic energy' that descends from above. In his view, the earth is spinning on its axis, and we are pushed toward the surface by the resulting centrifugal force. This is a very attractive idea. One almost wishes it were the correct explanation. But there's the testimony of the astronauts, and, of course, Mr. Navarro's numbers are wrong.[11]

With a little college physics we can show that for gravity to have the power it does, and for it to result from centrifugal force, and for the earth to be 8,000 miles in diameter, it would have to be spinning at about 26,000 feet per second, and that is just a little fast. The earth is actually spinning at about 242 feet per second. If we use that figure and we make Mr. Navarro's assumption that gravity is centrifugal force, we find that the earth could only be 1,830 feet in diameter for gravity to be as powerful as it is. The whole land surface of the earth (the inside surface, that is) would be only about three tenths of a square mile!

The earth is obviously bigger than that – in fact, my back yard is bigger than that – and that being the case, I think we can safely consign Mr. Navarro's theory to the same scientific Siberia as the push-pull theory, the 'aetherial shower' theory, the inside-out theory. Is there no hope?

Well, there is, but to find it you will have to really put your thinking cap on. There is one other theory that I have not discussed yet that is somewhat more difficult to shoot down. In fact, it is somewhat more difficult to build up. This theory was proposed by a man who towers above all the rest of us intellectually to such a degree that it seems almost blasphemous to even suggest that he could ever be wrong. Cambridge PhD's mention his name in awe. Princeton undergraduates once prayed to sit at his feet. He was an expatriated German named Albert Einstein.

Einstein's theory was based on a principle that was implied in Newton's Second Law of Motion. It is extremely simple, and it was there for all the world to see for two hundred or so years; but the world did not see it until Einstein came along. And if anyone had seen it, he probably would not have known what to make of it.

Newton's Second Law of Motion simply states that force equals mass multiplied by acceleration, and it is best understood by an example. Let us take the case of Sisyphus rolling his stone up a hill. We do not know just how heavy Sisyphus' stone really was, and for that matter we do not know the exact angle of the hill, or the coefficient of friction between the surface of the hill and the stone; but no matter. We shall just do what scientists do. If we do not know the numbers, we will make some up.

Let us suppose that to roll that stone up the hill, Sisyphus had to exert one hundred pounds of force. Now according to Newton's Second Law of Motion, if we know how massive his stone was, we can find out how fast he could get it up the hill before it rolled back down the hill and he had to start all over again. Let us say that his stone had one slug of mass. Now, according to Newton, one hundred pounds of force exerted against a mass of one slug means the stone would accelerate at a rate of one hundred feet per second per second. The problem is solved.

That means that when Sisyphus first started pushing his stone, its speed was zero feet per second. After one second the stone would be moving up the hill at one hundred feet per second. After two seconds the stone would be rolling at two hundred feet per second. No wonder Sisyphus was worn out!

When Sisyphus's stone started rolling back down the hill, the same laws of motion ruled its behaviour. But this time let us make the example a little simpler. Let us forget about what the Greeks said – we might as well, after all – and suppose that Sisyphus just dropped his stone from the Leaning Tower of Pisa, along with a grapefruit, just to see how fast they hit the ground.

As I said, Newton's Second Law governs what happens here, just as it did when Sisyphus was rolling his stone up the hill. In fact, it governs what happens whenever any kind of force acts on any kind of mass.

But there is one difference. When Sisyphus was rolling his stone up the hill, his rate of acceleration depended on the force he exerted on the stone and the mass of the stone (plus a few other factors I have ignored to keep this discussion simple, such as the slope of the hill, etc.). If we assume that his stone had a mass of one slug, then one hundred pounds of force would have resulted in one hundred feet per second per second of acceleration. More force would have resulted in more acceleration. The mass is constant here. But if Sisyphus dropped his stone and let it fall through space, the acceleration is constant.

Gravity causes an acceleration of thirty-two feet per second, no matter what is falling. That means that Sisyphus' stone would hit the ground at exactly the same time as his grapefruit, assuming, of course, that he dropped them both at the same time. And that simple fact is the basis for Einstein's theory of gravity. *There is a force of gravity, but gravity is not a force.*

What it is, is a tendency to cause things to accelerate toward the surface of the earth at the rate of thirty-two feet per second per second. It *produces* a force, but it is *not* a force.

Now, like all the other ideas I have discussed in this chapter, that one is likely to run against the grain of your habitual thinking. So let me dwell on this a little while before we go on. The force of gravity on anything is its weight. Thus, when we use Newton's Law, we can find the weight of anything by taking its mass in slugs and multiplying by thirty-two – the acceleration of gravity. So the stone of Sisyphus, with its mass of one slug, would weigh thirty-two pounds. It is that simple. An average man, with a weight of 160 pounds, would have a mass of 160 divided by 32, or 5 slugs. That means that weight is proportional to mass. And *that* means that everything that has a different mass has a different weight. A common observation. But if gravity was a force, the weight of everything would be the same, and it is not. The acceleration of everything is the same. Thus gravity is an acceleration.

To say that gravity is a force is the same thing as saying that petrol is energy. It produces energy, but it is not energy. The distinction is the same.

Now what this does is change the character of our basic question. No longer are we asking how it is that there is a force emanating from the surface of the earth that pulls us toward the ground. We are now asking how it is that there is a tendency for us to accelerate toward the surface of the earth at the rate of thirty-two feet per second per second. And it is precisely this change in the question that makes it possible for us to get an answer.

Not that the answer is simple. Einstein points out that speed, or velocity, to use scientific language, is simply how much space we can cover in a certain amount of time. And acceleration is the rate of change in our speed. Mathematically, changing speed to acceleration or acceleration to speed is merely a matter of one little mathematical operation. These two ideas are not the same, but they are kissing cousins. And that tells us that acceleration, like speed, is determined by measuring space and time.

Thus space and time are the two great yardsticks. But according to Einstein, they are not altogether reliable yardsticks. Because space and time depend on speed and acceleration, just like speed and acceleration depend on space and time.

One has to be really zipping along to notice, but when one goes faster, space starts shrinking and time slows down. That makes nonsense out of all our measurement systems, because as we increase in speed, space and time, which we use to measure speed, start changing. But as I said, you have to really be moving to notice and that is why nobody *did* notice. At least, until Einstein. If you are moving slowly, space and time do not change enough to inconvenience you. But they do change. In fact, space and time are different for every speed you take. And that leads to a chicken-and-the-egg situation.

We assume that because space starts shrinking when we go faster, our going faster causes space to shrink. But notice that word *assume*. What have I told you about that word earlier on? It is a very dangerous word. And there is really no reason for this assumption. One could just as well assume that the shrinking of space causes higher speed. And if you want to play a little philosopher's game, you can make another assumption. You can assume that if it was possible to somehow transcend the human condition and become omniscient, you would see that shrinking space and high speeds are the same thing – that, in fact, speed is *defined* by the shrinking of space. It may not look that way to us, but if you could assume this transcendent viewpoint you might discover that this is the correct interpretation after all.

As I said, acceleration and speed are kissing cousins. One mathematical operation is sufficient to turn one into the other. And that means that certain conditions in space are identical with acceleration, just as certain conditions in space are identical with speed. If we assume that those certain conditions can *cause* acceleration, then we have the explanation for gravity.

Einstein believed that the space surrounding the planet Earth is warped in some way that can be described using enormously complicated mathematical equations called tensors. This warping is caused by the presence of the planet in space. Empty space is not warped, but put something in it, and warping starts *ipso facto*. This warping is the kind of warping that would surround you or me if we were accelerating through space at the rate of thirty-two feet per second per second. And because of this warping we *do* accelerate through space at the rate of thirty-two feet per second per second. At least, we do if we are falling toward the ground.

This means that at the surface of the earth, space has actually shrunk relative to several hundred feet above the ground, and time has slowed down. Absolutely outrageous, isn't it?

Don't laugh, though, because since Einstein first proposed this theory in 1910, scientists have performed literally hundreds of experiments in an effort to bring it down. In every case the result has been the same – one more proof that Einstein was right. It may be that this German genius has finally resolved the age-old mystery of gravitation. But I might point out that there is nothing in all this that makes levitation impossible. And for the perceptive student, there is even a link with the occult. According to the theory of Vedanta philosophy, on which much Eastern occultism is predicated, time and space – the bases of gravity according to Einstein – are products of the mind of man. Thus, it may be that gravity is the product of man's creative consciousness and that in man's creative consciousness lies the secret whereby it may be overcome.

CHAPTER THREE

FAKIRS AND FAKERS

The fact that science cannot explain gravitation means that science cannot condemn levitation. So there is nothing unscientific about the occultist's claim that man can rise into the air through 'mere intention.' And that changes the character of our original question. It is no longer *can* man fly? but *does* man fly? And the evidence is that he probably does. Occasionally.

Of course, that does not mean just anybody can fly. Your next door neighbour probably cannot fly. And your boss probably cannot fly, either, although I don't recommend asking. But that does not mean flying is impossible. As William James said, it takes only one white crow to prove that all crows are not black. And it takes only one levitator to prove that all men are not earthbound.

'Levitation may be produced consciously or unconsciously,' writes Madame Blavatsky in *Isis Unveiled*.

The juggler determines beforehand that he will be levitated, for how long a time, and to what height; he regulates the occult forces accordingly. The fakir produces the same effect by the power of his will, and, except when in the ecstatic state, keeps control over his movements. So does the priest of Siam, when, in the sacred pagoda, he mounts fifty feet up into the air with taper in hand, and flits from idol to idol, lighting up the niches, selfsupported, and stepping as confidently as though he were upon solid ground. The officers of the Russian squadron which recently circumnavigated the globe, and was for a time stationed in Japanese waters, saw jugglers walk in mid-air from tree-top to tree-top, without support. They also saw the pole and tape-climbing feats, described by Colonel Olcott in *People from the Other World*. Quotations from Colonel Yule and others place beyond doubt that these effects are produced.[1]

Among primitive peoples, whose minds are unencumbered by the often unfortunate effects of modern rationalism, levitation is generally accepted. Dr. Imbert-Gourbeyre was told by a French missionary that the Indians in Oregon often practised levitation. More than once the missionary had seen with his own eyes the native shamans rise two to three feet from the ground and walk atop the blades of pampas grasses without bending the delicate panicles.[2]

In ancient Britain, it was universally believed that the Druids could fly, and there is some evidence that the secrets may not have been lost. In the thirteenth century, Friar Bacon is said to have walked in the air between two of the spires at Oxford. In his *Letters on Natural Magic* Sir David Brewster writes this off as an 'optical effect,' but it is difficult to see how the effect could have been produced.[3] And much the same can be said of the 'mechanical' explanation.

In one of his papers, Friar Bacon wrote that 'an instrument may be made to fly withal, if one sit in the midst of it and turn an engine by which the wings, artfully contrived, are made to beat the air after the manner of a bird's wings. By an instrument but three fingers high and three broad, a man may rid himself and others from all imprisonment.'[4] In another place, though, he says that he was not personally acquainted with the device itself, only with its inventor.[5]

That suggests that his feat of walking in the air at Oxford may have had a more esoteric significance.

In the case of the Tibetan sage Milarepa there is no question of any mechanical device. We read in the *Jetsun Kahbüm* that Milarepa acquired the flying siddhi after long hours of meditation on the 'third eye,' the Ajna Chakra, which is located between the eyebrows. When he learned that he could fly, Milarepa flew over the fields of a childhood neighbour, an old farmer, who was in the field ploughing with his son. The son saw Milarepa first, suspended in the air above them. But when he nudged his father, the old man was unimpressed.

'What is there to marvel at?' the old man asked. 'One Nyang-Tsa-Kargycn had a wicked son named Mila. It is that good for nothing starveling.'[6]

In her book, *With Mystics and Magicians in Tibet,* Mme. Alexandra David-Neel relates a similar story, with a note that such experiences are not uncommon among Tibetan mystics.[7]

They are not uncommon among mystics of other nationalities, either, but mystics from outside Tibet do not tend to think well of the siddhis. In *The Lives of the Philosophers* Eunapius says of the Greek Neo-Platonist philosopher Iamblichus that he was often seen by his servants to 'soar aloft from the earth more than ten cubits to all appearance.' When they told his disciples, the disciples asked the Master for a demonstration, whereupon he burst into laughter. Said he: 'He who thus deluded was a witty fellow, but the facts are otherwise.'[8] He did believe in levitation, though, because in his book on Egyptian sorcery, *On the Mysteries,* he warns against certain psychic manifestations, especially 'to appear elongated, or thicker, or be borne aloft in the air.'[9]

This attitude toward siddhis can be found throughout mystical literature. The siddhis exist – no one doubts that – but they must not be cultivated. In *The Yoga Sutras* Patanjali says that the siddhis are 'impediments to true perception.'[10] Certain Theosophists speak out against what they consider to be 'psychism' – the cultivation of psychic powers for their own sake. Ansari of Herat says in one of his writings:

Can you walk on water? You have done no better than a straw. Can you fly in the air? You have done no better than a blue-bottle.[11]

In *The Perennial Philosophy*, Aldous Huxley relates a story that appears in one of the Pali Scriptures (he does not say which one), and which has to do with the Buddha and levitation. It seems that the Buddha was lecturing on the sorrow of this world and the way to Nirvana when one of his disciples arrived and performed a 'prodigious feat' – such are Huxley's words – of levitation. Everyone waited for the Master to perform an even greater feat, but the Buddha only rebuked his disciple and continued lecturing.[12]

In the *Dighanikaya* Buddha explains that he discouraged the siddhis because they could be manifested just as well by non-Buddhists. Why should anyone become a Buddhist to perform levitation, when there were any number of saddhus and yogis around who could do the same thing? I suspect that there may have been another reason, though.

We must remember that the Buddha was the leader of his little group, and that his leadership depended on his ability to appear superior to his disciples. He had a political position to protect, and from that point of view, his disciple may have been guilty of *lese majesty*. If the Buddha could not perform an even *more* prodigious feat of levitation than his disciple, he would have had no choice but to rebuke him.

This comes out very strongly in the case of Iamblichus. We have seen that he was unable or unwilling when challenged to levitate for his disciples and that he tried to handle the situation through humour. But in a letter he wrote to his disciple Porphyry he was not laughing. He mentions people who 'have been known to be lifted up into the air' and he scoffs that 'the more ignorant and mentally imbecile a youth may be, the more freely will the divine power be made manifest.'[13] Iamblichus's inability to levitate was therefore proof of his superiority!

More ingenious masters have come up with more ingenious solutions. In one of his books, Bertrand Russell mentions an American religionist who told her followers she could walk on water. Naturally, someone wanted to see it done, and since there was no water at the spot where the challenge was made, she proposed to meet her disciples later at a nearby lake. The hour arrived, the followers were there, and when the lady showed up everyone expected a great show of levitation. Instead, they got a supreme test of their faith. 'How many of you believe that I can walk on water?' she asked. When they replied that they all did, she said that there was obviously no need for her to do it, and she walked away.

Levitation is not entirely unknown among mystics, though. According to Olivier Leroy, a Roman Catholic who wrote a long book on Catholic levitations, of the twenty thousand or so saints mentioned in the *Acta Sanctorum*, sixty or so were seen to levitate during their lifetimes.[14]

The most remarkable feats of levitation, however, were not performed by a Catholic saint but a Protestant sinner – Mr. Daniel Dunglus Home. 'There are at least a hundred recorded instances of Mr. Home's rising from the ground,' wrote Sir William Crookes.

> This has occurred in my presence on four occasions in darkness; but I will mention only those occasions when deductions of reason were confirmed by the sense of sight. On three separate occasions have I seen him raised completely from the floor of the room. On each occasion I had full opportunity of watching the occurrence as it was taking place.
>
> On one occasion he went to a clear part of the room, and, after standing quietly for a minute, told us he was rising. I saw him slowly rise up with a continuous gliding movement and remain about six inches off the ground for several seconds, when he slowly descended. On another occasion I was invited to come to him, when he rose eighteen inches off the ground, and I passed my hands under his feet, round him, and over his head when he was in the air.[15]

India is the true home of levitation, though, and it is in India that we will find more levitation stories than anywhere else. 'Levitation, or the rising of the body from the ground and its suspension a few feet up in the air above the seat or couch, is a universally accepted fact in India,' writes Ernest Wood. 'I remember one occasion when an old yogi was levitated in a recumbent position about six feet above the ground in an open field, for about half an hour, while the visitors were permitted to pass sticks to and fro in the space between.'[16]

In the third century, Prince Mahendra, a Buddhist, is said to have levitated to Ceylon with several of his followers, and to have alighted on Mount Missa. But that seems a little fanciful. More believable, and more typical, is what was reported by Apollonius of Tyana and his disciple Damis.

The story comes from *The Life of Apollonius of Tyana*, which was written by Philostratus and based on Damis's diary. The pair visited India during the first century, and, according to Damis, 'saw [the Brahmans of India] levitating themselves two cubits high from the ground.' Damis did not see anything particularly unusual in this, and neither, apparently, did the Brahmans. They did not perform levitation 'for the sake of miraculous display,' according to Philostratus. It was considered merely a simple act of piety to the sun-god.[17]

In a passage quoted by Colonel Yule, Friar Ricold mentions 'certain men whom the Tartars honour above all in the world, viz. The *Baxitae* [i.e. *Bakhshis*], who are a kind of idol-priests. These are men from India, persons of deep wisdom, well-conducted, and of the gravest morals. They are usually acquainted with magic arts, and depend on the counsel and aid of demons; they exhibit many illusions, and predict some future events. For instance, one of eminence among them was said to fly; the truth was (as it proved) that he did not fly but did walk close to the surface of the ground without touching it; and would seem to sit down without having substance to support him.'[18]

Something similar to this was also reported by Francis Valentyn. He says that,

A man will first go and sit on three sticks put together so as to form a tripod; after which one stick, then a second, then the third shall be removed from under him, and the man shall not fall but shall remain sitting in the air! Yet I have spoken with two friends who had seen this at one and the same time; and one of them, I may add, mistrusting his own eyes, had taken the trouble to feel about with a long stick if there were nothing on which the body rested; yet, as the gentlemen told me, he could neither feel nor see any such thing. Still, I could only say that I could not believe it, as a thing too manifestly contrary to reason.[19]

Contrary to reason, but not contrary to sense. Others have seen it done as well.

'When I appeared before Queen Victoria, at Balmoral, in 1878,' wrote Professor Kellar, 'I was asked if I could rival the feats of levitation which Her Majesty's officers in Northern India had observed and described in their letters home.

My reply was that with proper mechanical appliances I could produce an illusion of levitation and appear to overcome, as the jugglers did, the force of gravity, but that the actual feat of suspending the operation of that force was beyond my powers. As evidence of the world-wide curiosity manifested in these wonderful phenomena, I may mention the fact that the King of Burmah, when I appeared at Mandalay, and the venerable Dom. Pedro, in the Teatro Dom Pedro Secundo at Rio, made similar requests, to which I was compelled to return the same reply.

On the occasion of the visit of the Prince of Wales to Calcutta during the winter of 1875–6, I saw a marvel of levitation performed in the presence of the Prince and of some fifty-thousand spectators. The place was the Maidam, or Great Plaza, of Calcutta, and the old fakir who was the master magician of the occasion did his work out in the open plaza. Around him, in raised seats and on and under the galleries of the neighbouring houses, the native Princes and Begums were gathered by the score, arrayed in their silks and jewels, with a magnificence to which our Western eyes are little accustomed.

After a salaam to the Prince, the old fakir took three swords with straight cross-barred hilts, and buried them hilt downwards about six inches in the ground. The points of these swords were very sharp, as I afterward informed myself. A younger fakir whose black beard was parted in what we now call the English fashion, although it originated in Hindustan, then appeared and, at a gesture from his master, stretched himself out upon the ground at full length, with his feet together and his hands close to his sides, and after a pass or two made by the hands of the old man, appeared to become rigid and lifeless. A third fakir now came forward, and, taking hold of the feet of his prostrate companion, whose head was lifted by the master, the two laid the stiffened body upon the points of the swords, which appeared to support it without penetrating the flesh. The point of one of the swords was immediately under the nape of the man's neck, that of the second rested midway between his shoulders, and that of the third was at the base of his spine, there being nothing under his legs. After the body had been placed on the sword-points the second fakir retired, and the old man, who was standing some distance from it, turned and salaamed to the audience.

The body tipped neither to the right nor to the left, but seemed to be balanced with mathematical accuracy. Presently the master took a dagger with which he removed the soil round the hilt of the first sword, and, releasing it from the earth, after some exertion, quietly stuck it into his girdle, the body meanwhile retaining its position. The second and the third swords were likewise taken from under the body, which, there in broad daylight and under the eyes of all the spectators, preserved its horizontal position, without visible support, about two feet from the ground. A murmur of adulation pervaded the vast throng, and with a low salaam to the Prince, the master summoned his assistant, and lifting the suspended body from its airy perch they laid it upon the ground. With a few passes of the master's hand the inanimate youth was himself again.[20]

A more commonly reported version of Indian levitation is the Indian Rope Trick, which combines levitation with other performances that are, if anything, even more amazing. The account below is from Edward Melton, an Anglo-Dutch traveller, who saw the trick performed by Chinese conjurors in Batavia about 1670:

> I am going to relate a thing which surpasses all belief, and which I should scarcely venture to insert here had it not been witnessed by thousands before my own eyes. One of the same gang [of conjurers] took a ball of cord, and grasping one end of the cord in his hand slung the other up into the air with such force that its extremity was beyond the reach of our sight. He then immediately climbed up the cord with indescribable swiftness, and got so high that we could no longer see him. I stood full of astonishment, not conceiving what was to come of this; when lo! a leg came tumbling down out of the air. One of the conjuring company instantly snatched it up and threw it into the basket whereof I have formerly spoken. A moment later a hand came down, and immediately on that another leg.
>
> And in short all the members of the body came thus successively tumbling from the air and were cast together into the basket. The last fragment of all that we saw tumble down was the head, and no sooner had that touched the ground than he who had snatched up all the limbs and put them in the basket turned them all out again topsy-turvy. Then straightaway we saw with these eyes all those limbs creep together again, and in short, form a whole man, who at once could stand and go just as before, without showing the least damage! Never in my life was I so astonished as when I beheld this wonderful performance. It seems to me totally impossible that such things should be accomplished by natural means.[21]

'Hundreds of travellers have claimed to see fakirs [levitate] and they were all thought liars or hallucinated,' wrote Madame Blavatsky in *Isis Unveiled*.[22] James Webb concurs in *The Occult Underground*. After detailing several levitation episodes, he writes: 'There is no reason to doubt that these levitations *were seen to take place:* but it is also possible that occasions of extreme stress can well produce reports of such phenomena. For example, a French Dominican was seen levitated by one of the survivors of the wreck of the *Newfoundland* minutes before the ship sank in 1898.'[23]

If we are going to decide on the basis of historical incidents whether or not levitation is possible, we are going to have to sort those incidents out. There are several ways levitation can be simulated, and there are actual occult experiences that can easily be confused with levitation. I call these the 'not quite' categories of levitation stories, because they are not quite what they appear to be. The Indian Rope Trick is one of these. In *Beyond Telepathy* Dr. Indrija Puharich tells of a Dr. Rudolph von Urban who not only saw the very same feat described above by Edward Melton, but filmed it. Everyone agreed on the details – the rope was thrown into the air, the assistant's body was chopped up, etc. – but the film came out a little different. In the film two people walked onto the stage where the trick was performed, threw the rope into the air, and sat down for the remainder of the 'performance.' Using certain occult techniques that are known but extremely difficult to master, these fakirs had mesmerised the entire audience.[24]

Agehananda Bharati tells a similar story in his article in *Extrasensory Ecology*. In the early fifties, Mr. Bharati heard that there was a fakir in the Almore district of the Himalayas who was willing to levitate for anyone who was curious to watch. About fifty people showed up for the performance, including Mr. Bharati, and together they chanted the *kirtan*. Incense was burned under the full moon as the fakir went through certain yogic exercises. By six the following morning the crowd was well satisfied with what they had seen, but Mr. Bharati had seen nothing. When he spoke with some of the other spectators he learned to his astonishment that they had seen the fakir rise at least nine feet into the air. The fakir's name was Jairam Baba, and he had become famous in the area for his levitation demonstrations.[25]

Anyone who can mesmerise an entire crowd at pleasure possesses some occult powers, although levitation is not necessarily among them. But there is another way of simulating levitation that is simpler to learn and that is more widely practised. I call it stick levitation, because there is always a stick involved somewhere. A typical example of stick levitation can be found in Jacolliot's book on Indian occultism. The fakir in this case was named Coomaraswamy

> Taking an ironwood cane which I had brought from Ceylon, he leaned heavily upon it, resting his right hand upon the handle, with his eyes fixed upon the ground. He then proceeded to utter the appropriate incantations.
>
> Leaning upon the cane with one hand, the fakir rose gradually about two feet from the ground. His legs were crossed beneath him, and he made no change in his position, which was very much like that of the bronze statue of Buddha that all tourists bring from the Far East.[26]

A similar story appeared in the *Tatvabodhini Patrika* of March, 1847 and was translated for the August 1882 *Theosophist*.

> A few years ago a Deccan Yogi, named Sishal, was seen in Madras by many Hindus and Englishmen, to raise his *Asana*, or seat, up into the air. The picture of the yogi showing his mode of seating and other particulars connected with it may be found in the 'Saturday Magazine' on page 28. His whole body rested on the air, only his right hand lightly touched a deer-skin, rolled up in the form of a tube, and attached to a brazen rod, which was firmly stuck into a wooden board resting on four legs. In this position the Yogi used to perform his *japa* with his eyes half shut. At the time of his ascending to his aerial seat, and also when he descended from it, his disciples used to cover him with a blanket.[27]

In June 1936 *The Illustrated London News* published actual photographs of the trick being performed at a tea plantation in India. The yogi in this case was Subbayah Pullavar, and the photographer was an English tea planter named P. T. Plunkett. Once again the yogi was covered before and after the actual levitation performance, and once again a stick was involved.[28]

Now I cannot say for certain that any of these yogis were not actually levitating. They all may have been. But Sishal was later unmasked as a conjurer rather than an occultist, and there is an Indian levitation trick that is performed with a stick.[29]

The secret of the Indian levitation trick was first brought to Europe by the Oriental magician Ling Lau Lauro in 1826. Ling Lau Lauro preferred to use a bamboo stick, and, as D. H. Rawcliffe observes, 'the effect was impressive.'

'The secret of the trick,' Rawcliffe writes, 'was that inside the bamboo ran an iron bar bent at right angles at the top. Attached to this was a metal bracket to support the magician's body. The metal support and the horizontal iron stay were covered by the clothes and sleeves of the magician.'[30]

Sishal used a stool, but in most cases one end of the iron bar protruded into a hole in the ground that was of course prepared in advance and unseen by the spectators. Since some advance preparation was necessary, the trick could not be done just anywhere or at just any time. But it is not too difficult to do; too many travellers have seen it. And of course there was Robert Houdin, who 'levitated' his son on the Paris stage using this technique in 1849.

Not Quite Category Number Three is known in India, but better known in Europe. In the *Prabandhacintamani* the great yogi Nagarjuna is said to have acquired the flying siddhi from a certain elixir that he prepared.[31] In Europe these elixirs were known as the 'flying ointments,' and they played a great part in medieval witchcraft.

In his book *On Witchcraft*, published in 1533, Paul Grilland speaks of a trial held at Rome seven years before at which the defendant – a witch – was said to have practised levitation. It was said – and she did not deny it – that her flights always commenced when she rubbed a certain 'magic liniment' on her body.[32] In *The Book of the Sacred Magic of Abra-Melin the Mage* Abraham the Jew tells of a personal experience with the flying ointments:

> At Lintz I worked with a young woman who one evening invited
> me to go with her, assuring me that without any risk she would

conduct me to a place where I greatly desired to find myself. I allowed myself to be persuaded by her promises. She then gave unto me an unguent with which I rubbed the principal pulses of my feet and hands, the which she did also, and at first it appeared to me that I was flying in the air in the place which I wished, and which I had in no way mentioned to her.

I pass over in silence and out of respect that which I saw, which was admirable, and appearing to myself to have remained there a long while, I felt as if I were just awakening from a profound sleep, and I had great pain in my head and deep melancholy. I turned round and saw that she was seated at my side. She began to recount to me what she had seen, but that which I had seen was certainly different. I was, however, much astonished, because it appeared to me that I had been really and corporeally in that place, and there in reality to have seen that which had happened. However, I asked her to go alone one day to that same place, and to bring me back news of a friend whom I knew for certain was distant 200 leagues. She promised to do so in the space of an hour. She rubbed herself with the same unguent, and I was very expectant to see her fly away; but she fell to the ground and remained there about three hours as if she were dead, so that I began to think that she really was dead. At last she began to stir like a person who is waking, then she rose to an upright position, and with much pleasure began to give me the account of her expedition, saying that she had been in the place where my friend was, and all that he was doing; the which was entirely contrary to his profession. Whence I concluded that what she had just told me was a simple dream, and that this unguent was the causer of a phantastic sleep.[33]

Johannes Baptista Neopolitanus tells a similar story in his *Natural Magic*, although, unlike Abraham the Jew, he did not use the flying ointments himself.

There fell into my hands a witch who of her own accord did promise me to fetch an errand out of hand from far countries, and willed all them, whom I had brought to witness the matter, to depart out of the chamber. And when she had undressed herself, and froted her body with certain ointments (which action we beheld through a chink or little hole in the door),

> she fell down through the force of the soporiferous or sleepy ointments into a most sound and heavy sleep. So as we did break open the door, and did beat her exceedingly; but the force of her sleep was such, as it took away from her the sense of feeling, and we departed for a time. Now when her strength and powers were wearied and decayed, she awoke of her own accord, and began to speak many vain and doting words, affirming that she had passed over both seas and mountains, delivering to us many false and untrue reports.[34]

Neopolitanus believed that the flying ointments would not work with just anyone, but only with 'old women whose nature is extremely cold,' who are, in a word, melancholics. Judging from the nature of the ingredients, though, I would tend to say that the ointments *would* work with just anyone. They contain several dangerous drugs – difficult, but by no means impossible, to obtain. I do not recommend that anyone try them, though, because the same 'flights' can be had without danger, using purely mental methods.

Unfortunately, there's nothing unusual about this connection between drugs and the occult. Von Eckartshausen describes certain preparations that one can use if it is desired to see spirits, but he makes it plain that if you are not careful with them, you may join the spirits as well as see them. Likewise, Martinez de Pasqually, founder of the Martinist Order, is said to have used drugs to heighten the quality of experiences resulting from his theurgic experiments. But I cannot in good conscience recommend anything that I know to be extremely dangerous, and with that we come to Not Quite Category Number Four, which is a technique for flying without much risk of dying.

In *Psychic Discoveries Behind the Iron Curtain* Lynn Schroeder and Sheila Ostrander refer to an 'ancient saying that he who awakens the Anahat Chakra in the heart can walk on air.'[35] Now, as a matter of fact, that is not an ancient saying, but there are intimations to that effect in certain yogic books. And I suspect that the particular yogic book that inspired these two authors is

The Serpent Power, translated and edited by Sir John Woodroffe. In the description of the Anahat Chakra we read that by mastering this Chakra '[the yogi] is able to enter the enemy's fort or citadel, even though guarded and rendered difficult of access. And he gains power by which he may render himself invisible, fly across the sky, and similar powers.'[36]

This would seem to be a clear reference to an advanced form of levitation, but the same text contains a statement that the yogi 'is able at will to enter another man's body,' and that suggests something else. That suggests that what we have here is not a description of levitation at all, but another occult experience that can be easily confused with it – astral projection.

Anyone who has ever experimented with astral projection knows that one can indeed enter another man's body, or an enemy's citadel, 'even though guarded and rendered difficult of access.' But it is not necessary to worry with the Anahat Chakra in the heart to do astral projection.

There are a great number of astral projection techniques being offered by Silva Mind Control, Eckankar, the AMORC Rosicrucians, and a whole wad of would-be teachers who have presented their methods in books. But analysing all these techniques, we find that the key ingredient in every technique is the same – visualization.

The reason for this is that it is not really so difficult to project some ethereal vehicle of consciousness to a distant place. What is difficult is to maintain some continuity of awareness, so that you do not merely project to the place, but become aware of what is going on there.

Visualization helps here because one common centre in the brain is used for translating all kinds of psychic impressions into visual images. When you dream at night, or when you imagine something, or when you remember a past event, or when you become psychically aware of this or that, the same brain centre is at work. And you can easily prove this to yourself. If you start a programme of visualization exercises, you will find before long that your dreams become much more vivid and intense, that you can remember things more vividly, and that your psychic impressions, when they take the form of visual images, become much more clear and distinct.

If you want to try astral projection, let me suggest that you select a room where you can be alone for a while. Find a comfortable chair to sit in and position it so that you are facing either a bare wall or a wall with very few decorations. If it is necessary, you might want to move some of your furniture around, so that when you sit you have as simple and as unobstructed a view as possible. Now when you have achieved this, select some object that has a simple design and place it in the room so that it will be directly in your line of vision when you are sitting. I find that a table lamp that is painted in one colour or at most two colours works well for this. You don't want an extremely complicated painting, because that is too difficult to visualise – at least at first. And you do not want something that is too banal, because it won't present enough of a challenge to your budding powers. You want something that you can visualise accurately without undue effort.

Once you have selected your object, whether it is a lamp or whatever, put it where you will not see anything else when you look at it. Now sit down and study the scene in front of you. Take just a minute or two, and notice all the visual details, then close your eyes and try to 'see' the room and the object just as you did with your eyes open. This is a visualization exercise, but with a difference. When you visualise the room in front of you, you want to see it in your mind's eye just exactly the same way as you saw it with your physical eyes. You want to put your mental images 'out there' as it were, so that the wall of your visualised room seems to be the same distance in front of you as the wall of the actual room. The object that you have placed in front of you should be in your visualization just as far away as the actual object is. Now this may seem obvious to some of you, but I emphasise it because a common beginner's mistake is to put the mental images inside the head. If you want to achieve much success with astral projection you must surround yourself with your images, so that you 'see' the room the same way with your eyes opened or closed.

Now at first your images will fade quickly. This is to be expected, and, when it happens, you are to open your eyes, survey the room in front of you again so as to refresh your visual memory, then close your eyes and once again try to 'see' the room in front of you. Continue this exercise for ten to fifteen minutes at a session and try to have at least one practice session every day.

One thing that you will find in this type of development is that a brief session of ten or fifteen minutes a day will accomplish more for you than forty minutes to an hour every four days. After you have sharpened your powers of visualization somewhat, so that you are ready for something more complicated than a table lamp, let me suggest that you try a clock. Look at the clock, then close your eyes and rest for several minutes. Then visualise the clock in front of you. If you really are having any success in working toward astral projection, you will find that the clock you see in your mind's eye will show the correct time. Of course, that doesn't mean anything unless you allow some time to elapse between looking at the clock and visualizing it. But if you do some few minutes of meditation you will give the hands time to change position. As your practice improves, you may visualise a clock in a different room. Some students have worked with this experiment until they could instantly tell the correct time at any hour of the day without looking at a timepiece.

After about two weeks of this kind of practice, you may start having some spontaneous astral projection experiences. Don't expect too much at first. And especially don't expect to have instant control of the sort some Indian *mahatma* might have. But if you persist, you may find some evening as you are dropping off to sleep that you have the experience of 'stepping out' of your body just before you lose consciousness. These experiences will come most frequently in the late evening and in the very early morning, as you are just awakening, since it is at these times that the tension between the astral and physical bodies is weakest. Another experience that you may have is being able to actually see the room in front of you with your eyes closed, especially when you are meditating or after you have just awakened in the morning. At first these experiences will not be well developed; you will see, as Plato said, as if through a glass, and darkly. But in time you will be able to see better, and when you find that you can see clearly, even though the experiences are still spontaneous, you will be ready for your first astral step.

Your first trips will be quite brief. This is because the mind is still not well controlled, and if any doubt or fear enters your mind during an astral projection, you will find yourself immediately back in your body and unable to project again. You must learn, during projection, not to question anything that happens, unless you are clearly in danger from astral entities, else your experience will most definitely come to an end.

Now for a warning: there is a possibility – a remote possibility, to be sure, but a possibility none the less – that you may meet someone during one of your astral trips that you would rather shy away from. I tend to feel that one is more likely to be mugged walking the streets of a major city nowadays than meandering about on the astral plane, but the possibility exists. And some writers have blown this into something really ominous. A psychiatrist once associated with the Menninger Clinic has been quoted as saying, 'The persistent exploration in these realms . . . brings himself to the attention of the indigenous beings, who under normal circumstances pay little attention to humans . . . They are of many natures, and some are malicious, cruel, and cunning.'[37]

I shall not offer any comment on that, except to say that I have found in my own studies that some types of people are much more likely to have bad astral trips than others are. Astral projection, if you have never experienced it before, will challenge your current perceptions of reality in a way that you cannot imagine. It is also a very pleasant experience, but if you have ever had any emotional problems, and particularly if you have ever felt that your grip on reality is somewhat tenuous, you would be well advised to leave projection alone. That advice also holds if you have ever tried to deliberately become possessed with alien entities, either as a spirit medium or as a part of some magical ceremony or if you are a member of any religious sect that teaches the existence of demons or demon possession. If you do not recognise yourself in any of those descriptions, you should not have any problems during your astral voyages.

Now there is one 'danger' that some occult writers have mentioned that I consider to be completely nonsensical, and that is the possibility that your silver cord will get cut or tangled in some way during projection so that you cannot get back to your body. The silver cord is a sort of astral lifeline that connects your physical body with your roaming astral body during projection. It was first mentioned by Plutarch centuries ago, and has been seen occasionally by advanced students ever since. There is no doubt that it exists, but in most of your trips you will not even be aware of it. And I only know of one person who ever actually died doing astral projection – a fellow in New Jersey in 1972 who combined projection with some extremely dangerous experiments in suspended animation.

If you try this experiment and succeed, you will see how easily it can be confused with levitation. A beginner cannot get far doing projection, but the advanced student can easily travel thousands of miles in a second. The French Rosicrucian adept, the Comte de Chazal, is said to have witnessed all the horrors of the French Revolution from his home on the Isle of Mauritius.[38]

Many people have projection experiences and sensations of levitation at the moment of death, which is, after all, only a one-way projection to the astral plane. The Frenchman, Pieron, studied a number of dying people and found that these 'levitation' sensations are quite common. In most cases they are accompanied by a feeling of well-being, but Pieron mentions one girl who grasped the iron bars of her deathbed, apparently in mortal terror of something she 'saw' on the astral plane.[39]

If we can believe Dr. H. Spencer Lewis, late 'Imperator' of the Rosicrucian Order (AMORC), these experiences are not always subjective. In his book, *Rosicrucian Questions and Answers*, Dr. Lewis tells us that the 'heretic king' of Egypt, Akhnaton, experienced an actual levitation on his deathbed. Profane history has nothing to say about Akhnaton's demise, but Dr. Lewis claims privileged sources of information, and he says that late in the afternoon on a day in June 1350 BC, Akhnaton was seen 'to be actually raised for a moment and then to drop back in "sweet repose with a smile of illumination upon his countenance."'[40]

Occultists also call upon astral projection to explain the 'flying dreams' that many people have. In theory, our astral bodies get up and leave our physical bodies every evening while we are asleep, but because there is no continuity of consciousness between sleeping and waking in ordinary people, we are not aware of our experiences. On rare occasions, we can bring back memories of our astral experiences, and the result is the flying dream.

In an article on flying dreams, Havelock Ellis says that the French painter Raphael often had such dreams and then tried to fly after he awoke. 'I need not tell you,' said he, 'that I have never been able to succeed.'[41]

Others have, though. In the same article, Ellis mentions a French lady who could hover in the air for brief periods when she was wide awake. This is an experience that does not fit into any of our 'Not Quite' categories. The French lady was not using a stick; she was not sleeping; she was not projecting; and she was not using a 'flying ointment.' Moreover, she is not alone. Others have had the same experience. And that brings us to a problem that was first pointed out by Andrew Lang in *Cock Lane and Common-Sense*. Having considered a number of levitation stories, he asked:

When we find savage 'biraarks' in Australia, fakirs in India, saints in medieval Europe, a gentleman's butler in Ireland, boys in Somerset and Midlothian, a young warrior in Zululand, Miss Nancy Wesley at Epworth in 1716, and Mr. Daniel Home in London in 1856–70, all triumphing over the law of gravitation, all floating in the air, how are we to explain the uniformity of stories palpably ridicuous?[42]

There is only one explanation that I can see: some of the stories are true.

CHAPTER FOUR

A WORD WITH YOU

As I said in the last chapter, the book *The Serpent Power* connects levitation with the Anahat Chakra. The Anahat Chakra is one of seven psychic centres, or centres of psychic manifestation, in the human system, and although the 'levitation' mentioned in *The Serpent Power* is actually astral projection, nonetheless the Anahat Chakra is connected with levitation in other texts as well.

One of these is the *Siva Samhita*, which says that three chakras are involved in levitation: the Muladhara, the Anahat, and the Ajna. The Muladhara is located at the base of the spine, and the Ajna between the eyebrows, whereas the Anahat is located in the chest, in the vicinity of the heart, as we have said.[1]

To clairvoyants, these chakras appear to be swirling wheels of pure energy. In fact, the word 'chakra' literally means 'wheel.' They are centres at which certain occult energies in the human body are collected and concentrated. Properly aroused, they can produce extraordinary results.

One technique for properly arousing them is chanting. In *The Tarot*, Mouni Sadhu says of the fakirs that some of them 'have been able to raise themselves into the air for some time, just by the use of a certain sound, while being under special nervous tension. In other words, the fact, well known to occultists, of influencing matter by nervous force, is at work here.'[2]

The 'certain sounds' Mouni Sadhu refers to here are called mantras. The word is Sanskrit and, according to Bloomfield, means 'instrument of thought.'[3] The Egyptians called them the *hekau*, the 'words of power.'[4]

Lenormant speculates that the ancient Egyptians used these *hekau* to 'levitate' the great stone blocks of the pyramids into place. He points out that with the machinery that was available in ancient times (or our times, for that matter) it would have been impossible to transport these blocks from distant quarries to where the Pyramids were located within any reasonable period of time, and it would also have been impossible to seat them as accurately as they were seated. Impossible, that is, unless some occult forces were at work.

The Egyptians believed that the *hekau* were the secret names of powerful deities. The profane names of the gods were known to everyone, but their secret names were known only to the initiated. It was believed that by means of these secret names the deities could be bound and forced to do the will of the magician. Origen tells of an inferior branch of Egyptian magic that was based on the names of daemons.[5] A similar theory, based on the names of angels instead of gods, found its way into the magical lore of the Qabalah.

In some cases, the most efficacious names were found to be those that were popularly known, and, in these cases, severe penalties were exacted from anyone who thoughtlessly spoke the name of the god aloud. One of these was 'Amen,' the name of the sun-god of Thebes, which was chanted by Theban priests to evoke the god to visible appearance. As Plutarch says in *Isis and Osiris:*

> When they, therefore, address the supreme god, whom they believe to be the same as the Universe, as if he were invisible and concealed, and implore him to make himself visible and manifest to them, they use the word 'Amen.'[6]

Such are the boons to be acquired from mantras. Now this word – Amen – is used in Christian liturgy. Yet the sun-god does not appear. How so?

Yogis say that it is because the word is not chanted properly. They say that the first syllable of Amen should be pronounced AUM, so that the word itself is pronounced AUM-EN, whereas it is now generally pronounced AHH-MEN. It is from the first syllable of the word that the word gains its occult power. AUM is recognised as a powerful mantra in the East as well as the West.

The word AUM, chanted aloud, stimulates the Ajna Chakra, the chakra located between the eyebrows. In Hindu tradition, this chakra is said to be an organ of psychic sight. It is called the 'third eye,' or the 'eye of Shiva.'

This is why the Egyptian priests were able to get visual manifestations by chanting AUM. It is very doubtful that the god Amen ever existed. But by opening the third eye, these priests would have seen bright white lights or possible visions of celestial beings.

In Hindu tradition, the three letters A, U, and M are said to represent the three persons of the Hindu Trinity: Brahma, Vishnu, and Shiva. They also represent the three realities of Time: Past, Present, and Future, and the three states of awareness: waking, dreaming, and sleeping. AUM is the Inexpressible Absolute, the last word to be spoken in mysticism, after which there is only silence.

It is also the lost word, or, to borrow a phrase from the *Sepher Yetzirah*, 'the articulate word of creative power' – the Logos, the Word that built the worlds. Advanced yogis are said to hear the sound of AUM psychically, which signifies to them that it underlies all Creation.

The three sounds of AUM, the A, the U, and the M, together represent all the sounds that the human voice can make. A originates in the throat, and M is made with the lips, whereas U, according to Swami Vivekananda, 'represents the rolling forward of the impulse which begins at the root of the tongue until it ends in the lips.'[7] It is every sound in nature, and birds and animals are said to understand it.

I tried this last tradition out on my cat. Ordinarily she does not mind my mutterings and sputterings, but when I draw out the word AUM, softly but distinctly, she runs and hides under the bed. I have decided that she probably lacks the true mystic temperament. She probably will not get far on the Path.

Now in Sanskrit it is correct to consider the AU as a diphthong, and pronounce it as a single sound, but all authorities are agreed that when the mantra AUM is chanted, the A, the U, and the M must each be chanted separately. Thus we make the AHHHH sound, then gradually fade into the OOOOO, and then finally fade out with the MMMMM. Each of these sounds has power taken by itself, but they must be combined and combined in the proper sequence to have the greatest effect.

Mantras can be chanted mentally as well, and that brings us to a different channel within the same tradition.

It is difficult to say just how old mental chanting is. A mental technique is described in the medieval mystical text called *The Cloud of Unknowing*, but it is doubtful that mental chanting was widely in use in Europe much before the thirteenth century. The technique does have some striking benefits, however, and it does not appear to matter what word one uses for a mantra.

The English poet Lord Tennyson used this technique, with his own name for a mantra. In a letter to B. P. Blood, as quoted by William James, he says:

A kind of waking trance – this for lack of a better word – I have frequently had, quite up from boyhood, when I have been all alone. This has come upon me through *repeating my own name to myself silently*, till all at once, as it were out of the intensity of the consciousness of individuality, individuality itself seemed to dissolve and fade away into boundless being, and this not a confused state but the clearest, the surest of the surest, utterly beyond words – where death was an almost laughable impossibility – the loss of personality (if so it were) seeming no extinction, but the only true life. I am ashamed of my feeble description. Have I not said the state is utterly beyond words?'[8]

Utterly beyond words it is, but Tennyson was not afraid to try again to explain the state, this time in a poem:

For more than once when I sat alone,
Revolving in myself
That word which is the symbol of myself,

The mortal limit of Self was loosed,
And past into the Nameless, as a cloud
Melts into Heaven. I touched my limbs,
The limbs were strange, not mine
And yet no shadow of doubt,
But utter dearness, and through loss of Self
The Gain of such large life as matched with ours
Were Sun to spark, unshadowable in words,
Themselves but shadows of a shadow-world.

In *The Power of Positive Thinking*, Dr. Norman Vincent Peale calls this the 'technique of suggestive articulation,' and offers some advice of his own on how to do it: 'Repeat audibly some peaceful words,' he writes. 'Words have profound suggestive power . . . Use such words as "tranquillity." Repeat that word slowly several times. Tranquillity is one of the most beautiful and melodic of all English words, and the mere saying of it tends to induce a tranquil state.'[9]

I have personally found it quite effective to chant the word 'peace' to myself over and over again. The word has the proper vibratory qualities to make a good mantra – its vibrations are soothing and peaceful – and the concept that the word represents perfectly describes the meditative state that mantra chanting is intended to produce.

Those who have followed the meditative scene at all probably know that mantra chanting is also the basis for Transcendental Meditation, as taught by the Maharishi Mahesh Yogi. Like the authors quoted above, the Maharishi Mahesh Yogi instructs his students to repeat a mantra to themselves over and over again until they reach the meditative state.

There is one difference, though, between the Transcendental Meditation technique and those that have gone before. According to TM teachers, one must have just the *right* mantra. In his *Meditations* Maharishi explains that mantras are of real value only if 'the qualities of the energy impulses created by the sound of the mantra rightly correspond to the energy impulses of the man ... Any wrong choice of the mantra is sure to create unbalance in the harmony of the man's life.'[10]

This view is also given out by Maharishi's disciples. In *TM: Discovering Inner Energy and Overcoming Stress* we read that: 'The danger of using a mantra of unknown effect is dramatized by numerous reports from people who have used nonsense syllables, euphonious sounds, or words with pleasing meanings. In every case, meditation with these mantras was less favourable than the correct practice of the TM technique.'[11]

One of the authors, Dr. Harold Bloomfield, tells us in his book on *Happiness* that 'a person will think his mantra to himself many thousands of times in his life and in doing so will trigger a whole constellation of changes. To disregard the need for a mantra which will produce only life-supporting effects is foolish and possibly dangerous.'[12]

TM students receive one mantra each at the time of their initiation, but it is difficult to get one to tell what his mantra is, because they believe that the mantras will lose their power. One TM meditator told me that if he spoke his mantra aloud, its power would be dissipated throughout the universe and that it would become useless. Another explained that the mantra would be brought from 'inner consciousness' to 'outer consciousness' and lose its power that way.

I am inclined to rather doubt that these theories are correct, and so, apparently, are some meditators. In an article in *Atlantic* and also in his book *Powers of Mind*, Adam Smith discloses his mantra – SHIAM. Three other TM mantras can be found in the November 1975 issue of *Time* magazine – SHERIM, IMA, and INGA. William Whalen, writing in *U.S. Catholic*, adds two more – RAM KIRIM and SHRI RAM. Thus, at least six TM mantras have been made public in national publications. There are others of more dubious authenticity to be found in other sources.[13]

Even if you know what the mantras are, though, that information is said to be useless unless you also know how they are selected. Not every TM meditator gets the same mantra. Instructors explain that the process is personalised, that each meditator receives a mantra at the time of his initiation that was especially selected just for him when he was initiated into TM.

Exactly how this works, though, most instructors will not tell. Lawrence Domash alludes somewhat hazily to 'a set of objective rules that (the instructor) is trained to apply,' and his boss does not go much further than that. In an interview with *Life* magazine, Maharishi said that, 'A skilled teacher can [select mantras] easily by asking questions about the person's health, feelings, education, profession, and marital status.'[14]

There are intimations here and there that the process might be quite difficult. In his *Meditations*, Maharishi says that 'there are thousands of mantras and all have their specific values, specific qualities, and are suitable for specific types of people.'[15] One instructor emphasised to me that several months of training were required to become a teacher. How then, he asked, could I expect to grasp these things in a moment?

According to instructors who have left the movement, it would not be difficult at all. There are indeed thousands of mantras, but only sixteen are parcelled out to new meditators. Which one of the sixteen you get depends on your age at the time of your initiation.

One complete list of TM mantras, together with the age groups for each mantra, was published in 1977 in an uncopyrighted circular by the 'Spiritual Counterfeits Project' (SCP) of the 'Berkeley Christian Coalition' – an anti-TM organization in California. The SCP list also appears in appendix 1 of John Weldon and Zola Levitt's *Transcendental Explosion*, where we are told that its accuracy has been verified by two former instructors connected with the SCP. Two additional lists were published by Mr. Frank Kaleda of Kent, Ohio, in a privately printed manuscript called *The Shining Ones*. And still another list was published by Nicholas Regush in his column in the May 21, 1978 *Sunday Express* (Montreal). This last list was given to former TM instructor Susan Scott in 1973 and was obtained from her husband, R. D. Scott, also a former TM instructor and the author of *Transcendental Misconceptions*.

All of these lists contain the same mantras, with some differences in spelling since the mantras were originally given out orally. All of them contain exactly sixteen mantras, and all of them are arranged according to age. There are some differences in sequence from one list to the next, but by comparing several lists it is possible to arrive at a consensus. The following list is an effort to reconcile all the other lists:

Age	Mantra	Age	Mantra
0–11	Eng	26–29	Shiring
12–13	Em	30–34	Shirim
14–15	Enga	35–39	Hiring
16–17	Ema	40–44	Hirim
18–19	Ieng	45–49	Kiring
20–21	Iem	50–54	Kirim
22–23	Ienga	55–59	Sham
24–25	Iema	60+	Shama

After you have been initiated and have received your mantra, you are eligible for an 'Advanced Technique' that is supposed to speed your progress toward Cosmic Consciousness. The Advanced Technique is just another mantra. Thus, if you were originally initiated at age thirty, your mantra would have been *Shirim*. Then, if you received the Advanced Technique, your mantra would have become *Shri Shirim*. According to some sources, meditators using the Advanced Technique are advised to lengthen their meditation period to one hour, instead of the twenty minutes used by beginners.

After you have been using the Advanced Technique for a while, you become eligible for still another Advanced Technique.

This, like the first one, is just another mantra, so that if you have received your first Advanced Technique and your mantra is *Shri Shirim*, your second Advanced Technique will transform your mantra into *Shri Shirim Namah*. Says Mr. Kaleda of Ohio: 'Other advanced techniques may be used, but of six initiators questioned, it was always the prefix *Shri* and the suffix *Namah*.'[16]

That leads some people to believe that the mantras may be the names of Hindu gods, because the words *Shri* and *Namah* have definite meanings. In a book entitled *The Holy Tradition*, which is given to TM initiators during teacher training courses, the word *Shri* is translated 'Oh, most beautiful,' and the word *Namah* is translated 'I bow down.' That means that rendered into English the Advanced Technique mantra says 'Oh, most beautiful Shirim, [to you] I bow down.' In Alain Danielou's *Hindu Polytheism* the words *Aim*, *Hrim*, *Srim*, and *Krim* are mentioned as being related to various Hindu gods, and, as we see, they are also similar to certain TM mantras. *Aim*, which is quite similar to *Iem*, is used in the worship of Sarasvati, the Hindu goddess of knowledge.[17]

That connects TM directly with the Hindu traditions in which it is rooted and reveals the true reason why the mantras must be selected by a teacher.

It is not that the mantras are difficult to select; they obviously are not. But there is a tradition in the *Mantra Shastras* that for a mantra to be efficacious it must be received from a guru who stands in line of descent from the ancient masters, having received the mantra from his guru, and so on. Failing that, the tradition holds that one must perform an esoteric ceremony, the details of which are known in the East, which is said to bring the mantra to life as it were. It appears that the TM initiation ceremony is designed to achieve just this result.

According to a pamphlet issued by the Spiritual Counterfeits Project, the initiation ceremony is carried out in an incense-filled room, wherein is a small table, atop which is a picture of Maharishi's dead master, Guru Dev. When the new meditator enters the room, he removes his shoes and presents his initiator with three gifts: fruit, fresh-picked flowers, and a clean, white handkerchief. The fruit and flowers are placed on the handkerchief and all three of these are placed beneath the picture of Guru Dev. The initiator then kneels and chants a Hindu song called *puja* in which he offers homage to all the masters in the Shankara tradition.[18]

According to the SCP pamphlet, the *puja* is itself a mantra. By chanting it, the initiator puts himself and the person he is initiating in a peculiar state of awareness, in which the new meditator's mantra can be deeply implanted in his consciousness. That is why the mantra is given immediately after the puja has been sung. And it is also why a mantra received during a TM initiation is considered more effective than a mantra one simply chooses for oneself. In emphasizing this point, the SCP pamphlet points out that the new meditator is advised, just after receiving his mantra, to let it 'dwell' in his consciousness. 'The fact is that the mantra can "dwell" there,' says the pamphlet, 'because it has been *placed* there by traditional ceremonial techniques.'[19]

So there you have it. There is obviously some value in going through the formalities of actually receiving a mantra in an initiation, but I think it unlikely that using a non-TM mantra, or even using a TM mantra without being initiated, will have all the bad effects that Maharishi and his followers claim. And Dr. Benson, author of *The Relaxation Response*, argues that a non-TM mantra is likely to be just as effective.

'We believe it is not necessary to use the specific method and specific personal secret sound taught by Transcendental Meditation,' writes Dr. Benson. 'Tests at the Thorndike Memorial Laboratory at Harvard have shown that a similar technique used with any sound or phrase or mantra brings forth the same physiological changes noted during Transcendental Meditation.'[20]

One of these physiological changes results in a feeling of extreme bodily lightness, or even weightlessness, the first stage in levitation. At the turn of the century, a psychologist named Lydiard H. Horton became quite interested in this effect and tried to induce it in several experimental subjects who had no training in meditation. These subjects were given a simple relaxation technique that was not as powerful as the mental mantra chanting technique, yet the results were striking:

'One of [the subjects] jumped out of the chair,' wrote Horton, 'and was afraid to continue the experiment; so realistic was his apperception of a soaring motion.'

'Another, this time a woman, gripped the chair in the momentary belief that she was floating away; two others reported that they felt "caught up by a wave."'

'One other enjoyed the sensation so much that he took it as a matter of course. One other said if his head had been as light as his body he would surely have floated away. He reported himself "just floating away," the sensation being overwhelmingly real.'[21]

In *The Secret of the Golden Flower*, as translated by Richard Wilhelm, this experience is described in more typically Oriental language: 'When one is sitting in meditation the fleshly body becomes quite shining like silk or jade. It seems difficult to remain sitting; one feels as if drawn upward.'[22]

Horton characterises the experience as 'the illusion of levitation,' but *The Secret of the Golden Flower* disagrees. Says the text: 'In time, one can experience it in such a way that one really floats upward.'

To do this, choose a mantra for yourself, either your first name, or your last name, or one of the TM mantras, or whatever. It hardly matters what you use, although I don't recommend that you use AUM or OM. This is an excellent mantra, but it is usually chanted in a slightly different way than we are going to chant our mantra, and I suspect it is best not to mix the techniques.

I also do not recommend that you use a meaningful word with negative connotations. If you want to chant the word 'peace' to yourself, fine and good. But do not use a word like 'kill' or 'war.' Traditionally, mantras contain one, or at most, two, syllables, but you may feel free to use more if you wish. After all, Tennyson's mantra, 'Tennyson,' had three syllables. But you should not use a word that is so complex that you have to use a great deal of intellectual effort to chant it. 'Honorificabilitudinitatibus' is a perfectly good *word*, but a perfectly lousy *mantra*!

Now for position. We are going to try some yogic *asanas* later on, but for now I just want you to sit upright in a straight-backed chair with some light padding for your seat and no padding whatever in the back. Separate your legs; place your feet on the floor in front of you about one foot apart; and place your hands, palms down, on your knees. Take a deep breath, and as you expel it, close your eyes and relax. Remain in this relaxed position, with your eyes closed, for a minute or a minute and a half, then start repeating your mantra to yourself slowly. Continue this for ten to fifteen minutes, and you are through!

When you are finished, do not open your eyes immediately. Stop repeating your mantra for a few moments, then stretch your arms as you would if you were disembarking from a long train ride. Give your body a chance to return from the quieter levels of awareness to the level of activity – otherwise you may wind up with a headache. If you have difficulty opening your eyes after your meditation session, do not be alarmed. This is a natural reaction. It simply means that you are not yet ready to return to the level of activity and that you should do a few more moments of stretching and possibly take a few deep breaths before resuming your normal activities. Remember, what you are doing here is not hypnosis. There is no need to fear that you will get lost in meditation, as some people think, or that you will be subjugated to anyone else's will, or any of the other strange things that people sometimes come up with. This is a very natural technique and extremely beneficial. If you suffer from allergies, high blood-pressure, migraine headaches, or any other specifically stress-related ailments, you may find some relief in this practice. You will not want to use this technique after eating or before retiring in the evening. The very best time for it is early in the morning before starting your day. That way the benefits will be with you all throughout the day.

If you perform the technique properly, before long you should experience the weightlessness feelings that I have mentioned. You may feel that all the weight has gone out of your body, or you may feel that you are about to float away. Some people have the sensation of being suspended a couple of feet in the air.

Once you have acquired this sensation, which is very common among experienced meditators, I want you to imagine that your right arm is composed of light tufts of cotton down. Do not make an effort to do this, because if you do, the effort that you make will interfere with the process of meditation. Just start your mantra, and when the weightless feeling comes over you, imagine that just your right arm has become extremely light, that it is not even made of flesh but that it has become magically transformed into cotton. And imagine furthermore that you have attached a balloon filled with hydrogen gas to your arm with a string and that the balloon is pulling your arm into the air. This technique is known as 'hand levitation' and is valuable because it tells you how easily you will master certain later exercises and also because it deepens the trance established by mentally chanting your mantra. One person who tried this experiment wrote:

> The hand would float up into the air without the slightest effort on my part. This was such a strange experience that my consciousness was drawn in from the world around me. I was so fascinated with the floating of my hand that my mind remained free of ordinary concerns.[23]

People with a special talent for hand levitation can cause their hand to rise four inches into the air after only thirty seconds of concentration. But I must caution you not to lift your hand if you want results. The hand should simply rise of its own accord. Later we will try the same thing with the entire body.

CHAPTER FIVE

ASTRAL ENERGIES

One of the earliest levitators in history was a Samarian magician named Simon Magus. He was the heir of an occult school started by another Samarian named Dositheus, and in many ways he was the spiritual ancestor of P. T. Barnum.

He loved show. Dressed in his magnificent Oriental head-dresses and flowing robes, Simon would prowl the ancient streets of Samaria introducing himself as a god, and his girl-friend, actually an exprostitute he met in the city of Tyre, as the reincarnation of Helen of Troy.

He was the master showman, and if he had lived a century earlier, his life would have been without controversy. But this was the first century AD. The Christians were just getting started then, and Simon's self-deification caused them to take umbrage. They challenged Simon to a long series of theological debates, which make extremely boring reading in the original, and which ended the way long theological debates always end – inconclusively.

At that, Simon decided to move the contest to a different plane by performing a few miracles. He rightly considered that the masses would understand a miracle far better than theolog-ical theories.

He made his way to Rome, where he might perchance catch the ear of the emperor, and upon arrival lost no time in assem-bling a large crowd. Said he:

'Tomorrow, about the seventh hour, you shall see me fly over the gate of the city in the form in which you now see me speak-ing to you.'

And with that he left. Now, Rome's amusements were many, but there was nothing to compare with this, and when the seventh hour arrived on the morrow, the spectators were not absent. In time, the magician appeared, and what happened after that may be found in the apocryphal *Acts of Peter*:

> Suddenly a dust was seen afar off in the sky, like a smoke, shining, with rays stretching far from it. And when he drew near to the gate, suddenly he was not seen; and thereafter he appeared, standing in the midst of the people.[1]

Other accounts have it that he levitated from a platform, or in Rome's great amphitheatre, but all of them agree on one point: that a levitation was performed. And in one of Simon's manuscripts, he tells us how it was done.

Simon's manuscripts were preserved after his death by a group of occult scholars called the Simonians. Most of the manuscripts dealt with his peculiar cosmogonical theories, but a few dealt with practical occultism. And the particular manuscript in which the secret of levitation is described was translated by the alchemist Malchus in the fourteenth century.

Now before I present the text to you, let me say that although the secret of levitation is described, it is not clearly described. It is written, as the mystics say, both within and without. It conceals more than it reveals, but with the help of Eastern sources, we can wrest from it most of its meaning:

'Simon,' says the text, 'laying his face upon the ground, whispered in her ear: "O Mother Earth, give me, I pray, some of your breath, and I will give thee mine; let me loose, O Mother, that I may carry the words to the stars, and I will return faithfully to thee after a while."

And the Earth, strengthening her status, none to her detriment, sent her Genius to breathe of her breath on Simon, while he breathed on her; and the stars rejoiced to be visited by the Mighty One.'[2]

An odd little passage, isn't it? And yet notice the repeated references to breath and breathing. They are not so odd. In the Far East, says Swami Vivekananda, 'there are whole sects trying to [lighten] the whole body by withdrawal of breath and then they will rise in the air.'[3] The control of breath for occult purposes is the basis of an entire science, called *pranayama*, and levitation is only one of the benefits that are said to accrue therefrom.

In fact, according to Professor Harry Kellar, certain fakirs in India use a technique that is almost identical to Simon's, laying their faces upon the ground, breathing of their breath upon the earth, and receiving the breath of the earth in return.

'I have heard in India that the fakirs walk in the air,' wrote Professor Kellar, 'but I have never been a witness of the feat; the accounts given me came second or third hand, and related that the magician laid himself flat upon the earth, face downwards, for a minute or a minute and a half, then arose, and, pressing his arms tightly against his sides, stepped forwards and upwards as if upon an aerial stairway, walking up into the air to an altitude of several hundred feet.'[4]

Somewhere Pope seems to speak of this, when he writes: 'He mounts the storm; he walks on the wind.' But Pope was a poet; he did not have an explanation for levitation. Professor Kellar does:

My informant said he thought this might be done through an occult knowledge of electrical currents, as if these fakirs changed at will the nature of the electrical current with which their body was charged from negative to positive, or vice versa, inhaling an electrical influence from the earth which had the effect of destroying the force of gravity.[5]

This is considered *the* explanation of levitation in the Far East. There are others, as we shall see, but this is the most favoured. And there is a somewhat more extensive treatment of the theory in Madame Blavatsky's *Isis Unveiled*:

The starting point here is the electro-chemical principle that bodies similarly electrified repel each other, while those differently electrified mutually attract. 'Chemistry,' says Professor Cooke, 'shows that while radicals of opposite nature combine eagerly together, two metals, or two closely allied metalloids, show little affinity for each other.'

The earth is a magnetic body; in fact, it is one vast magnet, as Paracelsus affirmed three hundred years ago. It is charged with one form of electricity – let us call it positive – which evolves by spontaneous action in its interior. Human bodies, in common with other forms of matter, are charged with the opposite form of electricity – negative. Now what is weight? Simply the attraction of the earth. 'Without the attraction of the earth you would have no weight,' says Professor Stewart. How can he get rid of this attraction? The condition of our physical systems, say theurgic philosophers, is dependent on the action of our will. Well regulated, it can produce 'miracles,' among others, a change of electrical polarity from negative to positive. Man's relations with the earth-magnet would then become repellent, and 'gravity' for him would cease to exist. It would be as natural for him to rush into the air until the repellent force exhausted itself, as, before, it had been for him to remain upon the ground. The altitude of levitation would be measured by his ability to charge his body with positive electricity. This control once obtained, alteration of his levity or gravity would be as easy as breathing.[6]

Quite literally as easy as breathing because, as we have said, it is through a special mode of breathing that this alteration of electrical polarity is brought about. The electrical energy in the air that Madame Blavatsky speaks of is called *prana* by the yogis – thus the name *pranayama* for the science of controlling it. Madame Blavatsky even believed that birds and fish use some sort of instinctive pranayama when they ascend in their respective environments. Writing in the August 1882 *Theosophist* in answer to some questions raised by an admirer in Salt Lake City, Utah, she said:

With birds and animals [it is] as instinctive a mechanical action as any other they execute; with man, when he thus defies the familiar conditions of gravity, it is something he can acquire, in his training as a Yogi. Though the former act unconsciously and [the Yogi] changes his polarity at will, the same cause is made operative, and both produce an identical effect. There are certainly alternating changes of polarity going on in the bird while ascending or dropping, and a maintenance of the same polarity while sailing at any given altitude.[7]

In a different place in *Isis Unveiled*, Blavatsky returns to the same theme. 'The levitation of the adept,' she says, 'is a magneto-electric effect. He has made the polarity of his body opposite to that of the atmosphere, and identical to that of the earth; hence attractable by the former, retaining his consciousness the while.'[8] It must be said, though, that there is another interpretation, not only of levitation, but of the way that fish rise and fall in the sea. T. H. Huxley deals with this one, only half sarcastically, in *The Nineteenth Century* literary publication:

Theoretically, therefore, we can have no sort of objection to your miracle, and our reply to the levitators is just the same. Why should not your friend 'levitate'? Fish are said to rise and sink in the water by altering the volume of an internal airreceptacle, and there may be many ways science, as yet, knows nothing of, by which we who live at the bottom of an ocean of air may do the same thing. Dialectic gas and wind appear to be by no means wanting among you, and why should not long practice in pneumatic philosophy have resulted in the internal generation of something a thousand times rarer than hydrogen, by which, in accordance with the most ordinary natural laws, you would not only rise to the ceiling and float there in quasi-angelic posture, but perhaps, as one of your feminine adepts is said to have done, flit swifter than train or telegram to 'still-vexed Bermoothes,' and twit Ariel, if he happens to be there, for a sluggard? We have not the presumption to deny the possibility of anything you affirm – only, as our brethren are particular about evidence, do give us as much to go upon as may save us from being roared down by their inextinguishable laughter.[9]

In occult science, this 'something a thousand times rarer than hydrogen' that Huxley mentions, presents no problem at all. Science recognises three states of matter, but occult science recognises seven. Hydrogen is merely a gas, the third state of matter according to ordinary chemistry. If one could find the same element – hydrogen – present in the atmosphere in the fourth state instead of the third, then naturally it would be a thousand times rarer. Presuming that one could then draw this fourth state of hydrogen into the human system, through *pranayama*, and retain it there, there would be no reason why the body would not rise in the air like a hydrogen-filled balloon.

There is another possibility, though, that deserves our consideration also, and that is that we do not actually take in a gas a thousand times rarer than hydrogen, but that we affect the atmosphere surrounding us in such a way as to produce the same effect.

A hot-air balloon rises in the air by virtue of the fact that the hot air inside the balloon is rarer than the cooler air outside. Hot air rises and carries the balloon with it. Now man is surrounded by an energy field – occultists call it the human aura. Suppose – I am just speculating now – that this aura can be strengthened or modified in character in some way so that the density of the surrounding air is altered thereby. The Adept would in those circumstances be surrounded by an invisible balloon the size of his auric emanations, within which the air would be rarer than it would be outside. It is not impossible that under these conditions the Adept would be lifted into the air, along with his aura and the invisible balloon that his aura creates. He would rise in the air the same way a swimmer, his lungs filled with air, rises in the water. There would be nothing mysterious about it, just a simple question of buoyancy.

There is still another possibility that emerges from the nature of *prana* itself. We have already said that levitation comes from *pranayama*, and that *pranayama* comes from control of an energy in the air called *prana*. Now in Vedantic philosophy, as interpreted by Swami Vivekananda, there are only two basic realities in nature: *prana* and *Akasa*. *Akasa*, which literally means 'space,' albeit space in a certain philosophically special sense, is the occult basis of matter. All matter proceeds from *Akasa*, or space, according to what the *Siva Samhita* calls the 'order of subtle emanation.' In the same sense, *prana* is the basis for all movement and force and energy. As such, *prana* is energy in its purest form, before it becomes any particular *kind* of energy. And, as such, *prana* is all kinds of energy.

'*Prana* means force,' wrote Vivekananda, 'all that is manifesting itself as movement or possible movement, force or attraction ... electricity, magnetism, all the movements in the body, all the movements in the mind – all are the various manifestations of the one thing called *Prana*.'[10]

A few pages after that the Swami broadens that definition somewhat. He says that '*prana* is gravitation,' and with that we connect with levitation.

If we follow Western physics as laid down by Sir Isaac Newton, the very act of rising in the air, by whatever means, involves energy, and in fact raises us to a higher energy state. When we fall to the ground, all we are doing in Newton's view is going from a higher energy state to a lower energy state. And there is by implication nothing absurd in the idea that by taking in energy, in whatever form, we could rise by nonmechanical means.

Now most people who have not studied Newton's theories have only a very nebulous idea of what the word *energy* really means, and if we are going to see clearly how Newton's ideas pertain to levitation and explain the connection between *prana* and levitation, we are going to have to have a very clear idea. In Newton's mechanics, energy is simply force acting through a distance.

Suppose that you have awakened in the morning and discovered that your car will not start. Suppose, furthermore, that you decide to push it to the nearest garage. If you have to exert two hundred pounds of pressure on the rear of the car to get it to move, that is force. But if you exert that two hundred pounds and move the car two feet, that's energy. You have exerted a force through a distance. And, in fact, we get the amount of energy by just multiplying the force and the distance through which it acts. Thus, two hundred pounds of force through two feet of distance is two hundred times two, or four hundred foot-pounds of energy.

Now it makes no difference what direction the force is acting in; but if I pushed the car upwards, away from the ground, for the car to move, I would have to exert a force equal to or greater than the force with which gravity pulls it toward the earth. In other words, I would have to push upward with three to four thousand pounds of force, whatever the weight of the car is. And in this case, the energy involved is called *potential energy*.

I weigh one hundred seventy-five pounds. That means that if I rise in the air one foot, I have exerted one hundred seventy-five pounds of force through a distance of one foot, thereby expending one hundred seventy-five foot-pounds of energy. The higher I go, the greater the energy expended, although the force involved will never be greater than my own weight. That is why it is more difficult to levitate two feet into the air than it is to levitate a foot.

Now the important point here is that this energy must be taken in from somewhere before the rising process can start and that is where *prana* comes in. *Prana*, as we have said, is gravitation, but it is also every other form of energy. In a passage that echoes that of Swami Vivekananda, Swami Vishnu Devananda explains that:

Prana is also known as universal energy. It is *prana* that is manifesting itself as gravitation, electricity, as the actions of the body, and as the nerve currents and thought force. From thought down to the lowest physical force, everything is thus the manifestation of *prana*.[11]

Since *prana* becomes all forms of energy, it follows that it can be transformed into all forms of energy, including mechanical energy and even potential energy, the kinds of energy one needs for levitation. But enough speculation. It is just about time for us to forget about the why and concentrate on the how. In the next chapter I shall tell you how to actually rise into the air, so that you can perhaps contemplate these mysteries from a loftier perspective.

CHAPTER SIX

SOME PRACTICAL SECRETS

In the *Digha Nikaya*, Buddha says of the Adept that 'he walks on water without sinking into it, as if it were solid ground; his legs crossed and bent beneath him, he journeys through the sky like birds on their wings.'[1] Similarly, Sanang Setzen, as quoted by Colonel Yule, lists ten marvellous powers that were attributed to the yogis of his time, among them flying and 'sitting in the air with legs doubled under.'[2] Both of these are references to levitation, of course, but they also refer to a specific posture that must be assumed when doing levitation. This is the cross-legged position. It is sometimes called the 'Buddha posture' because the Buddha is usually shown sitting in it, but its proper name is *Padmasana* – the full lotus. Says the *Siva Samhita*:

> When the yogi, though remaining in *Padmasana*, can leave the ground and rise into the air, then know that he has gained *Vayu-siddhi*, which destroys the darkness of this world.[3]

This is a fairly simple posture for Hindus and for people with extremely slender legs. Most Europeans and Americans find it rather difficult, though. In fact, for some people, getting into the full lotus is almost a 'siddhi' in itself.

Nevertheless, *Padmasana* is essential for the serious student of levitation. Not only is it traditional; it is difficult to imagine a better posture to be in when you descend. Almost any position will do on the way up, but what goes up must come down – levitators are no exception – and your initial landings are likely to be rather bumpy. Having your legs secured, which you do when you assume *Padmasana*, minimises the likelihood of injury.

To do *Padmasana*, sit on the floor and extend both legs straight in front of you. If need be, you may lean backward slightly for comfort. Now bend your right leg and bring your right foot *over* your left thigh. Not under – over. If you did that properly, your right foot and perhaps the lower pan of your right ankle should be resting atop the uppermost part of your left leg. Now comes the fun part. Leaving your right foot where it is – no cheating, now – bend your left leg and bring your left foot over your right thigh. Congratulations! You are now sitting in the full lotus.

Or are you? Unless you have studied yoga before, or unless you are quite young or unusually limber, I suspect that you are either sitting in the half lotus or in the Western sloppy-cross-legged position, with your feet tangled loosely below your legs. If that is the case, you have some work to do.

Anybody can get into the half lotus, with one leg crossed and one leg uncrossed, and that is our starting point for developing the flexibility we need for the full lotus. Sit on the floor again, legs extended straight in front of you, and this time bring just your right leg over your left thigh. Now stop. You have just assumed the half lotus. Just to be correct, you might want to fold your left leg under your right leg, which is quite easy to do. Now place both your hands, palms downward, on your right knee, and press your right knee gently down toward the floor. The object here is to stretch these joints, so that they gradually become more limber. After a few minutes of stretching the right knee joints, uncross your right leg and do the same with your left leg. Fold your left leg over your right, place your palms on your left knee, and S-T-R-E-T-C-H.

After a few weeks you will acquire enough limberness in your knees to assume the full lotus itself, even if only for a short time. From time to time as you continue practising the half lotus try the full lotus. Once you have acquired the ability to get into the full lotus briefly, you will find that you will make much better progress using it than using the simpler posture.

If you find that one knee is more flexible than the other, cross it first, then cross your less flexible knee. You will find that it works easier this way than the other way. And by all means avoid pain. Yoga is not a painful system, although I once studied under a *Kundalini* instructor who *thought* it was. If your knees hurt an hour after you finish practising, you are overdoing it. You will be wise not to do any more *asanas* until the pain goes completely away and any soreness in your knee and hip joints is completely healed.

Once you manage the full lotus, simply sit in the posture for a few minutes every day. Especially at first, do not do any extra stretching. The posture itself will do all the stretching that is necessary. As time goes by you will find the posture comes easier and easier, until eventually you sit quite comfortably in it and use it for meditation.

You may take consolation from the fact that the more difficult the lotus is to do, the more you need to do it. Yogis say that old age is just the loss of suppleness in the joints. By twisting yourself into the Oriental pretzels yogis call *asanas*, you keep your joints limber long after other people will have begun to have problems. Some advanced students have maintained a youthful appearance into their seventies, largely by just doing the *asanas* on a regular basis.

Once you've acquired *Padmasana*, cup the back of your head in the palms of both your hands, and, with legs crossed in the full lotus, slowly lean backward, leaving your knees touching the floor, until your shoulders touch the floor behind you. This is *Masyasana*, the 'Fish Posture.' It is very easy to do once you have acquired *Padmasana*, and it is worth doing in itself for the stretching it gives to the vertebrae in your back and for the special stimulation it offers to your thyroid gland.

Now that you know how to sit, the next step is to learn how to breathe. Neither of these is very esoteric. Most people have sat on the floor at some time in their lives, and everybody who is alive is breathing. But there is a special way of sitting if you want to do levitation, and there is also a special way of breathing. The way we breathe in yoga is called *diaphragmatic* breathing. I call it D-breathing for short.

Sit in the full lotus, or the half lotus, if you gave up on the full lotus; place your right hand on your chest, and your left hand on your stomach. Breathe naturally, and as you breathe, notice which hand moves, or if both hands move. If your right hand moves you may have work to do, and if your left hand doesn't move, you definitely have work to do. Your left hand is just about where your diaphragm should be, and ideally it is the only hand that should be moving.

Still sitting in the full lotus, draw a deep breath, and draw it in by pushing the wall of your stomach outward, thereby creating a vacuum in your lungs. This is called the 'Pot-shaped' in yoga, because your body assumes the shape of a pot – a stigma in society but highly desirable in yoga. Hold your breath as long as is comfortable, then force it out of your lungs by pulling your stomach in and decreasing the capacity of your lungs.

This is the only natural way to breathe, which is probably the reason why most people have to be taught to do it. Practise the technique for ten or fifteen minutes until you have the idea, then forget it. Your body will assert its natural wisdom and you will do D-breathing forever, without even thinking about it.

After you think you have acquired this technique, the next step is to learn systematic deep relaxation. The reason for this one will be obvious after you have learned it: when you are relaxed it is easier to get your breathing under control.

If you live close to a swimming pool or some body of water that is suitable for swimming, there is a very easy way to prove this to yourself. I call it the 'underwater meditation.' Take a deep breath, immerse yourself completely in water, and see how long you can hold your breath. With a little experimenting you will see clearly that the more relaxed you are, the easier it is to hold your breath for an extended period.

This experiment will not lead to any great occult development, but I highly recommend it to anyone who has never tried it. There's no more effective way to demonstrate to yourself the value of relaxation in connection with measured breathing exercises. If you do not have a body of water available, you may achieve some of the same results by immersing your head in a bathtub, but the underwater meditation is most effective if your entire body is immersed several feet below the surface.

To do systematic relaxation, you will need to sit upright in a straight-backed chair that has no padding. Sit as you would sit for meditation, with your legs uncrossed, hands resting loosely in your lap, eyes closed. You will not want to sit in *asana,* at least not at first. You do not want your body twisted about or made uncomfortable in any way when you first attempt this exercise.

The technique itself was developed by Edmund Jacobson at Harvard in 1908. It is a Western technique, but it mixes well with Eastern methods and has become a staple of meditation and psychotherapy classes.[4]

Simply sit in the chair, close your eyes, and become aware of the muscles in your feet. Try to sense the condition that those muscles are in, and *will* that they should relax. Some people find it helpful to first tense the muscles, to give themselves an idea of what tension feels like, and then relax them. After you have released the tension in your feet, do the same thing with the muscles in your ankles, then your calves, and so on until you reach the top of your head.

After you have completed a cycle of relaxation, beginning with your feet and ending with the top of your head, start over again with your feet. You will find the first few times you try this that by the time you start relaxing the muscles in your head, your foot muscles are starting to grow tense again. After the second or third cycle, try to feel waves of relaxation sweeping from the bottoms of your feet to the top of your head, over and over again, and as you feel each wave of relaxation, mentally say the word 'relax,' exhaling as you do so.

This exercise is a lot like *asana*, in that the more difficult you find it to do, the more you need to do it. It is a good exercise to remember during meditation, for there will come a time during your meditation that you will feel an irresistible urge to return to the world of activity. This indicates that some inner tension is rising to the surface, and that inner tension can be released using the systematic deep relaxation technique.

The exercise may also help you if you have any breathing difficulties that are tension related. Certain kinds of allergies and sinus problems that make *pranayama* impossible exist only because of tension. If you suffer from these kinds of problems, you will know if they are tension related because the systematic deep relaxation exercise will cause the symptoms to disappear completely. When this happens, tell yourself that you will be able to maintain this state of relaxation even after you have arisen from your chair and gone about your other affairs. And when you tell yourself this, say it with the knowledge and conviction that it is true. You will not succeed on the first try, but in time you will be able to maintain this relaxed condition permanently. I have managed to cure myself of severe allergies using this very technique.

After you have practised with the relaxation exercise and you have acquired the feeling of relaxation, you will be able to instantly relax your entire body, merely by the desire to do so. The systematic technique will no longer be necessary. Learning to relax is just like any other manual skill. Once you have learned it, you can do it automatically.

Now to combine relaxation with *asana*. Sit in *Padmasana*, close your eyes, and feel the waves of deep relaxation sweeping through your body. Once you feel that you are relaxed, begin to notice the rhythm in your breathing. The more relaxed you are the slower this rhythm will become.

Now, maintaining your state of relaxation and sitting in *asana*, plug your left nostril with your left thumb and breathe in through your right nostril. Continue inhaling until you have acquired as much air as you can comfortably hold, then use your right thumb to plug your right nostril. Now start counting slowly from one to one thousand, and when you have held your breath as long as you comfortably can, remove your left thumb and exhale slowly through your left nostril. When you have exhaled all your breath, without straining or forcing, begin inhaling again slowly, this time through your left nostril. After you have inhaled as much as you can comfortably hold, hold your breath with your left thumb plugging your left nostril. Start counting again, but this time start exhaling when you reach the same count you reached on the first cycle. Then, remove your right thumb from your right nostril and exhale through your right nostril.

Now for some words of advice: when you inhale, inhale only as much air as you can comfortably hold. If you fill your lungs to bursting point, which is a very common mistake with beginners, you will find yourself gasping for breath on the exhale cycle. Remember, when you exhale, you must exhale S-L-O-W-L-Y. Anything that interferes with your ability to exhale slowly is incorrect performance of the technique.

Another word of advice is, under absolutely no circumstances hold your breath beyond the limit established on your first *pranayama* cycle. When you hold your breath the first time, remember the count you reached when you felt you needed to start exhaling and do not exceed that count in subsequent cycles. Pranayama can block the accumulation of carbon dioxide in your blood and foul up nature's system for letting you know when you need more air. If you do not heed this advice, you may literally mangle yourself unawares.

The three phases of a *pranayama* cycle, inhalation, breath retention, and exhalation, have Sanskrit names that we shall use from here on. Inhalation in yoga is called *Puraka*; breath retention is called *Kumbhaka*; and exhalation is called *Rechaka*. The object of *pranayama* practice is to gradually extend the length of time you spend in *Kumbhaka*, but this process must be undertaken very gradually. As the *Hatha Yoga Pradipika* warns:

> Just as lions, tigers, and elephants are controlled by and by, so
> the breath is controlled by slow degrees; otherwise it kills the
> practitioner.[5]

All the ancient yogic texts recommend starting out with twenty cycles of *Puraka*, *Kumbhaka*, and *Rechaka* per session. I have found that this takes about five minutes, which means that you can do it under almost any circumstances without interfering with your normal schedule. If you perform *pranayama* four times a day – once in the morning, once at noon, once in the evening before dinner, and once before retiring – you will have spent no more than twenty minutes a day doing *pranayama*. Yet the results may be dramatic.

Some of the results traditionally described are that the eyes shine, the complexion becomes absolutely clear, breathing becomes particularly easy, and the body becomes extremely light, as if one could levitate. These are signs that the *Nadis* – thousands of psychic nerve channels within the human system – are being purified. You should reach this stage within three months.

If possible you should start doing *Pranayama* during one of the mild seasons of the year – spring or autumn. If you have taken a meal, you should wait one hour before starting *pranayama*, four hours if the meal was a heavy one. If your stomach is empty (i.e. upon awakening in the morning), you will want to take about eight ounces of milk with possibly a slice of buttered toast before practising.

Before long you will start to have certain experiences, which are traditionally described in the *Siva Samhita*:

> In the first stage of *pranayama* the body of the yogi begins to
> perspire. When it perspires, he should rub it well, otherwise
> the body of the yogi loses its *dhatu* [humours]. In the second
> stage, there takes place the trembling of the body; in the third,
> the jumping about like a frog; and when the practice becomes
> greater, the Adept walks in the air.[6]

These same stages are also mentioned in *The Gheranda Samhita*, where they are related to three levels of advancement in *pranayama* practice:

By practising the lowest *pranayama* for some time, the body begins to perspire copiously; by practising the middling, the body begins to quiver (especially in the area of the spinal cord). By the highest *pranayama*, one leaves the ground, i.e., there is levitation.[7]

The lowest *pranayama* is called the *Adhama*, the middling is the *Madhyama*, and the highest is the *Uttama*. The difference between them is in the time spent in doing *Puraka*, *Kumbhaka*, and *Rechaka*. The texts give precise ratios of times for each of these phases of *pranayama*, and these ratios are called the PKR ratios, or the Puraka-Kumbhaka-Rechaka ratios.

According to Vasu's translation, for *Adhama* twelve seconds should be spent doing *Puraka*, forty-eight seconds doing *Kumbhaka*, and twenty-four seconds doing *Rechaka*. That gives us a PKR ratio for *Adhama* of 12:48:24, the numbers referring to the number of seconds spent doing *Puraka*, *Kumbhaka*, and *Rechaka* respectively. The PKR ratios for *Madhyama* and *Uttama*, according to the same translation, are 16:64:32 and 20:80:40.[8]

In *The Serpent Power*, Arthur Avalon quotes from the same text, but apparently from a different translation. In his version, the PKR ratios for *Adhama*, *Madhyama*, and *Uttama* are respectively 4:16:8, 8:32:16, and 16:64:32, and are based on the number of mental repetitions of the *pranava* mantra. The pranava mantra is AUM, although you may prefer to use the short form OM for pranayama. One hundred *Uttamas*, according to Avalon, results in levitation.[9]

If you use a mantra chanting technique to time your *pranayamas*, you may want to make yourself a rosary. That allows you to perform the necessary counting, but without expending any intellectual effort which might interfere with the alteration in consciousness that will result from the technique. I personally prefer to use a length of very light rope in which I have tied a series of knots, although others will prefer beads on a string.

Even without keeping track of the times, you will probably start perspiring fairly quickly. The next sign of progress is trembling, and here I must issue a warning.

Trembling is a sign that *Kundalini* is being awakened. *Kundalini* is a mysterious force or energy that is said to originate at the base of the spine and that is symbolised by a serpent, coiled three and one-half times. Somehow I have had all the *Kundalini* experiences that have been noted by authorities on the subject without any undue difficulty. But others have not been so lucky. Dr. Theos Bernard's experience is typical:

First there appeared the itching sensations. As I continued to practise, the sensation increased. Soon I began to feel as though bugs were crawling over my body. While I was working my legs would suddenly shake. Later, other muscles unexpectedly contracted, and soon my whole body would shake beyond control.[10]

If you start to have negative experiences of any kind while doing yogic exercise, remember that the experiences are brought on by doing the exercises, and can be discontinued by discontinuing the exercises. When you make it to the 'trembling' phase in *pranayama*, I would strongly suggest that you make contact with a yoga instructor and maintain the contact until the trembling passes. If you have not mastered *asana* by this time, you might want to discontinue your *pranayama* exercises for a while until you learn to sit in *Padmasana*. This posture will help you keep the trembling under control.

If you make it through the trembling stage, eventually you may arrive at the third stage, the 'jumping about like a frog.' The *Siva Samhita* calls this *Darduri-Siddhi*, the 'frog-jump power.' It is said to come from contemplation on the Muladhara Chakra, which you will recall is one of the three chakras traditionally associated with levitation.[11]

In another place the same text calls it the *Bhuchari-Siddhi* and says that 'through the strength of constant practice [in *pranayama*] the Yogi ... moves as the frog jumps over the ground, when frightened away by the clapping of hands.'[12]

This frog-jumping, or, as it is more commonly called, 'Hopping,' is the first stage of outward success in levitation. It is simply a brief rising into the air, and it is explained by the fact that the body, meaning presumably the pranic current in the body, is not balanced. Thus instead of rising straight into the air and remaining there for some time, you rise up and move forward at the same time, coming down again some distance away. When your body is balanced, a stage very few people ever achieve, you will be able to hover. As a TM-Sidhi course instructor explained to me: 'Maharishi says that you have to crawl before you can walk, and walk before you can run. In levitation you have to hop before you can hover, and hover before you can fly.'

Flying I'm a little sceptical about. But hovering has been achieved by some people, and hopping is a demonstrable fact. 'There is no doubt whatever about this phenomenon,' writes Aleister Crowley, 'It is quite common.'[13]

Different people experience hopping in different ways. In *Higher Psychical Development*, Hereward Carrington says that for him, hopping was a felt tendency to rise, rather than an actual rising itself. 'This is a peculiar feeling if you are sitting cross-legged,' he writes. But Aleister Crowley had a more advanced experience.[14]

Crowley experienced the trembling stage as 'an automatic rigidity of the muscles' and hopping as 'the very curious phenomenon of causing the body, while still absolutely rigid, to take little hops in various directions. It seems as if one were somehow raised, possibly an inch from the ground, and deposited very gently a short distance away.'[15]

Instructors in the TM-Sidhi Programme, who bring about hopping with slightly different methods, report that it is not unusual for people to rise one to three feet and move forward six to ten feet before coming down again. *Paramahansa Yogananda* saw this phenomenon performed by the 'levitating saint,' Nagendra Nath Bhaduri. Says he: 'A yogi's body loses it grossness after certain *pranayamas*. Then it will levitate, or leap about like a hopping frog.'[16] His colleague in yoga, Mr. I. K. Taimni, does not even see anything odd about it:

> No one imagines that the law of gravitation is violated when a rocket soars into the air. Why should it be necessary to assume that a miracle has happened when a man rises into the air by means of *pranayama*? . . . Levitation is a very common phenomenon in *pranayama* practice and is due to the pranic currents flowing in a particular way.[17]

To prove to you that hopping is a physical possibility, I would like to introduce you to a little levitation experiment that I call Party Levitation, since people used to use it as a party game. I first learned about it in a very unusual place – the lift of an office building in a major American city. Since then I have seen it performed several times, usually by people who were doing it for the first time, and I've never seen it fail.

To do Party Levitation you will need five people, one to be levitated – henceforth to be called the levitat*ee* – and four to do the levitating – henceforth to be called the levitat*ors*.

The levitatee sits in a chair and the four levitators stand around him so that they form a square. One levitator should stand to the levitatee's left, and just behind his left shoulder. Another levitator should stand in front of him and to his left, close to his left knee. The other two levitators should stand on the right side of the levitatee's body and in similar positions.

Now the object of Party Levitation is to make the levitatee's body so light in weight that the four levitators can lift him several feet into the air using a single finger each. If the experiment is performed properly, none of the levitators will feel the slightest resistance to their efforts. It will be as if the levitatee's body had lost its weight entirely.

While the levitatee is sitting, the four levitators surround him in the manner indicated and place their hands, one atop the other, on his head, as if they were healing him by the laying on of hands. While they are doing this, all of them will *will* mentally that the energy in the levitatee's body that causes him to be affected by gravity will be drawn out of his body. As Idries Shah interprets the experiment in his book *Oriental Magic*:

> The object here is to charge the subject with a negative electricity through the 'leakage' of human electricity provided by the other 'human batteries.' After several minutes, the effect of gravity can be proved to have been reduced. Two of the experimenters, using only two fingers, are able to lift the subject, chair and all.
>
> But the effect does not last long under these conditions. The static leaks into the earth. Thus the lifting must take place at once.[18]

Thelma Moss, who describes this experiment in *The Probability of the Impossible*, emphasises the need for the four levitators to lift in unison. To that end, you might want to have them lift on the count of three, or use some other device such as that.[19] If you do it properly, you will find that it works the very first time. And it is a startling demonstration.

Occultists say that the body of the levitatee becomes extremely light, perhaps even weightless, but that weightlessness alone is not enough to cause lift. One must have thrust to rise – a very small amount, to be sure, but thrust none the less. And that thrust is provided by the four levitators. The only difference between Party Levitation and *pranayama* hopping is that in hopping the yogi provides his own thrust.

If you persevere, you may be able to make the 'breakthrough' between hopping and hovering. It is a rare achievement, but by no means unheard of. ·

In his book *Secret Tibet*, Fosco Maraini tells a typical levitation story from the Far East. The levitator was an uncle of the

Princess Pema Chöki Namgyal of Sikkim, from whom Maraini got the story.

> He did what you would call exercises in levitation. I used to take him a little rice. He would be motionless in mid-air. Every day he rose a little higher. In the end he rose so high that I found it difficult to hand the rice up to him. I was a little girl and I had to stand on tip-toe. There are certain things you don't forget![20]

Indeed, it would be difficult for anyone to forget something like that! But lest anyone think that these things are seen only by little children, here is an account by Mr. Seenath Chatterjee, a man of undoubted integrity, who saw the performance as an adult, and who told his story in *The Theosophist:*

> For some weeks there was stopping in my house a Lama from Tibet, a true ascetic who daily practised his Yoga and spent hours, sometimes several days together, in meditative seclusion in the room I had assigned to him.
>
> I had found him one morning at my door begging his food after the custom of Buddhist religious mendicants, and, liking his appearance, asked him to come in. I had just taken him into the house and ordered food to be given him, when my milkman, a Bhootanese who spoke the Tibetan language, happened to call. Through him as interpreter I asked the Lama if he possessed any *siddhis*, or psychic powers. He enquired what phenomenon I should like to witness. I replied that it would be very instructive if I could see him rise into the air. He asked for a private room, called me in alone, shut the door, and drew the curtains before the window. Then, stripping off his clothing to the *languti,* or breech-clout, he took his seat upon an *asana*, or small board, that I had placed for him. Crossing his legs upon the thighs, close to the body – the usual posture of *Padmasana* in Yoga – he brought the thumb of each hand into contact with the ring-finger and, his hands against the abdomen, sat erect, turned his eyes upward, and remained for awhile motionless. His next action was to work his body with a wriggling motion, at the same time drawing several very deep breaths. After the third or fourth inhalation he seemed to retain

the breath in his lungs, and for a half-hour was as motionless as a statue of bronze. Then a succession of nervous shiverings ran through his body, lasting perhaps three minutes, after which he resumed his state of immobility for another half hour. Suddenly he, still retaining his sitting posture, rose perpendicularly into the air to the height of, I should say, two cubits – one yard, and then floated, without a tremour or motion of a single muscle, like a cork in still water. His expression was placid in the extreme, that of a rapt devotee, as described by eye-witnesses in the biographical memoirs of saints. After I had regarded him in amazement for at least a couple of minutes, I thought to myself that that was quite enough to satisfy my curiosity, and I hoped he would not give himself any more trouble on my account. At once, as though my thought had been read, he gently descended to his place on the *asana*. He then emptied his lungs by three or four strong expirations, opened his eyes, stood up as easily and naturally as though he had done nothing extraordinary, and laughed upon noticing my signs of bewilderment.

When he had resumed his clothing, the milkman was called in and the Lama bade him tell me that this sort of 'commonplace Siddhi' could be performed by even Lama-pupils in his Guru's monastery who were not very far advanced![21]

A similar story was told by Mr. Joshi Ootamram Doolabrahm, who was once Guru of the School of Astrology and Astronomy in Baroda. Mr. Doolabrahm encountered his guru in 1856, when he was trying to learn something of ancient Hindu theories about chemistry. After much searching, he tells us that he located an authority on that subject in the city of Broach, an ascetic attached to the temple of Mahadev, which was built on the banks of the river Narbada. The guru's name was Narayenanand, and he was a native of the Punjab. Writes Mr. Doolabrahm:

He was a man of about thirty-five years of age, above the average size of man, and with a beautiful countenance animated with a great intelligence of expression and cheeks suffused with a very peculiar roseate hue which I have never seen on any mortal's face before or since. His head was shaved, and he wore a saffron robe of a *sanyasi*. Like all men of his class, he was exceedingly difficult to approach, and would neither accept me as a pupil, nor allow me to put myself on terms of any intimacy until he had satisfied himself by the closest questioning as to my real intentions and capacity to learn the science of Yoga. I will pass over these details and simply state that, at last, I gained my object, was accepted as a pupil, received his blessing, and served him, first and last, for more than two years. During this time I learned many things practically, which I had previously known only from reading our sacred *Shastras*. I discovered many secrets of nature, my preceptor among other things practising *pranayam* [sic], sitting in the prescribed posture of *Padmasan* [sic], his body would rise from the ground to the height of four fingers, and remain suspended in the air for four and five minutes at a time, while I was allowed to pass my hand beneath him three or four times, to satisfy myself beyond a doubt that the levitation was a positive fact.[22]

So many people have seen hovering performed, especially in India, that it is impossible to doubt that it happens. But it is rare, far rarer than hopping. And the reason is quite paradoxical.

When levitation comes upon a person spontaneously, as it sometimes does with mystics, or occasionally with sick people, it is not uncommon for the person to hover in the air for thirty minutes to an hour or even more. But when an advanced yogi cultivates the ability to hover deliberately, a three or four minute levitation is quite an extraordinary achievement. Most people who assume this practice out of curiosity will do well to hover for a few seconds, or a minute at the most. Why this is nobody knows. But one thing we do know: it all has to do with certain altered states of awareness and the difficulty of maintaining those states of awareness deliberately. Levitation involves more than just the lungs; it involves the mind as well. And the mind is part of the next element in our technique.

CHAPTER SEVEN

THE ELEMENT OF WILL

In *Isis Unveiled* Madame Blavatsky writes that 'the Adepts of Hermetic Science explain the levitation of their own bodies by saying that the thought is so intently fixed on a point above them, that when the body is thoroughly imbued with the astral influence, it follows the mental aspiration and rises into the air.'[1] As before, this technique involves *prana* – 'the body is thoroughly imbued with the astral influence.' But it also introduces a new element – the element of will.

If we fill our bodies with *prana* they may become lighter in weight. And if we continue to work with *pranayama* exercises, our bodies may eventually leave the ground. But if we keep the exercises at purely a mechanical level, the results will be mechanical as well. In order to achieve complete success in levitation, the advanced student must learn to control *prana* with his mind.

This control is called 'Mind over Matter,' or 'Psychokinesis,' and it is possible because *prana* not only controls mind; *prana* is mind. There is, in fact, a Tibetan yogic treatise called *On the Identity of Mind and Prana* in which this fact is discussed at length.[2] In the *Hatha Yoga Pradipika*, another yogic treatise, we read:

> Mind and Breath are united together, like milk and water, and both of these are equal in their activities. Mind begins its activities where there is Breath, and Breath begins its activities where there is Mind.[3]

According to Evans-Wentz, the word *prana* exoterically means 'air, breath, energy, wind, vitality, propensity.' But esoterically it means an immaterial vital energy in the air that is to be distinguished from the material elements of the air and that man takes in when he breathes.[4]

Nor was this idea limited to the yogis. In *The Orphic Hymns* of Greece we read that 'the soul comes in from the whole when breathing takes place, being borne in upon the winds.'[5] The Greeks and other ancient peoples believed that virgins could be impregnated by the wind alone – so great was its connection with Mind and Soul – and that such was the origin of gods and heroes.[6] Jung points out that the Greeks had two words for wind. One of these, *pneuma*, also means 'spirit.' The other, *anemos*, is virtually identical to the Latin words *animus* and *anima*, which mean 'spirit' and 'soul' respectively. In Old Hochdeutsch, the Latin *spiritus sanctus*, which means 'holy spirit,' is rendered *atum*, which means 'breath.' Likewise, in Arabic the word *rih* means 'wind,' but *ruh* means 'soul.' Returning to the Greek, we have the word *psyche*, which means 'soul,' but which is closely related to such words as *psychein*, 'to breathe,' and *physa*, 'bellows.'[7]

In Jung's view 'these connections show clearly how in Latin, Greek, and Arabic the names given to the soul are related to the notion of moving air, the "cold breath of the spirits." And this is probably why the primitive view also endows the soul with an invisible "breath-body."'[8]

This 'invisible breath-body' came to be known later on as the *astral* body because it is influenced by the movements of the stars. But it is influenced by the movements of *prana* as well, and that is a fact that we shall find not only interesting, but useful and easily demonstrable.

We have only to think of how differently people breathe when in different states of mind. A person enjoying a good book breathes quite differently than a person enjoying sexual intercourse. The person who is reading will breathe quietly and rather slowly. This is characteristic of deep concentration, whereas the person who is having sex will breathe deeply and more rapidly.

There are also characteristic modes of breathing for all the other mental states as well.

Yogis say that when a person is angry, frightened, in love, concentrating, or whatever, there arises the *prana* of anger, fright, love, or concentration. For every mental state there is a corresponding state of *prana*, and at the moment of Enlightenment, when the yogi enters the state of *samadhi*, there is a radical transformation of *prana*, which results from the corresponding radical transformation in the mind.[9]

Alexander Cannon, who wrote *The Invisible Influence*, invented a device called the 'Cannon Psychometer' that he used to determine a person's state of mind by measuring the state of his breathing. The device was used to determine when a person was in the ideal state of mind for telepathic experiments. But it could also identify other states of mind as well.[10]

For example, it could determine how relatively excitable a certain person is. According to Mr. Ernest Wood, the average person breathes between twelve and twenty times a minute, and the more often he breathes – the more breaths per minute – the more excitable he is. Mr. Wood even extends this concept to animals. A hen, he says, averages about thirty breaths per minute, whereas a duck averages only twenty. This explains the obvious fact that both ducks and hens are more excitable than human beings, and that a hen is obviously more excitable than a duck. A monkey, according to Mr. Wood, averages about thirty breaths per minute, a dog twenty-eight, a cat twenty-four, a horse sixteen, and a tortoise three.[11]

Now if you were watching closely you may have noticed that relative excitability is also tied in with relative longevity. A dog has a shorter average life span than a cat, and of course the tortoise, slowest breather of all, is also one of the longest-lived animals.

This principle also applies to man. Hindu yogis say that every man is granted by karma a certain number of breaths, and that when that certain number of breaths is completed, the man dies. Now yogis say that man averages about fifteen breaths per minute, which comes to precisely 21,600 breaths in a twenty-four-hour day. If one could somehow slow down one's breathing, one could increase one's life expectancy.

That may be difficult to do without using special techniques, but something of the sort occurs during meditation. Mr. Wood says that in meditation a person's average rate of breathing may slow down to as little as six breaths per minute.

In an early experiment on TM meditators, published in the 27 March 1970 edition of *Science*, Dr. Keith Robert Wallace reported much the same thing. Briefly, a person who has been asleep for five hours or so usually reduces his oxygen intake (a good measure of respiration rate) by 10 to 12 per cent. TM meditators, on the other hand, who have meditated only a few minutes, reduce *their* oxygen consumption by as much as 16 to 18 per cent. This led Dr. Wallace to coin what has become almost a cliché in the world of meditation research – that TM produces a 'wakeful hypometabolic state.' Or, as one TM meditator put it to me: TM takes you 'deeper than the deepest sleep.'[12]

Your state of mind can also affect the way you breathe through your two nostrils, and here we connect the science of breath with practical yogic occultism. You will recall that in the last chapter I introduced you to an alternate nostril breathing technique. It may have seemed a little artificial at the time to plug one nostril and breathe only through the other, but in effect, we do it all the time without realizing it.

Yogis say that the left nostril is the passageway for the Moon Breath, whereas the right nostril is the passageway for the Sun Breath. Thus we have the name of Hatha Yoga, Ha-Tha, which means literally 'Sun-Moon.' The Sun Breath is supposed to be positive, masculine, and warm, whereas the Moon Breath is negative, feminine, and cool. The Sun Breath is said traditionally to be connected to the right trunk of the sympathetic nervous system via a psychic channel called a *nadi*, and the same is true of the Moon Breach. It is connected to the left trunk of the sympathetic nervous system via another *nadi*. These two trunks, the right and the left, are located physically on the right and left sides of the spinal column and are known as *Pingala* and *Ida* respectively.

Now this is important because at any given time either the Moon Breath or the Sun Breath is dominant, which means that we breathe much more strongly from the right nostril than the left, or vice versa. The nostril through which most of your breath is passing at any given time is called your dominant nostril in yoga, and it changes every two hours with certain tides on the subtler planes.

If it does not change every two hours, illness may be on the way. If your dominant nostril remains the same for a day, illness is certain. And if it remains the same for more than a day, the illness will be serious.

Also, if a man and a woman conceive a child, if both are breathing through the right nostril at the moment of conception, the child will surely be a boy. If through the left, it will surely be a girl. But if the man is breathing through one and the woman through the other, the child may be of either sex.

The next time you visit a friend and you do not know if he will be home, place your fingertips beneath your nostrils and breathe normally. If your right nostril is dominant, your friend will be home when you arrive. If your left nostril is dominant, he will not. The same thing is true of anything involving an element of chance. Yogis say that if your right nostril is dominant, the venture will be successful, but if the left is dominant, it will not.

The nostrils are also affected when you chant certain mantras. If you chant the mantra AUM aloud, and draw out the last sound, you may find that your breath flows more heavily through your left nostril than through your right. This is because the 'M' sound represents the feminine influence, and corresponds on the subtler planes to the quality of the Moon Breath. Dr. H. Spencer Lewis, who points this out in a magazine article, adds that 'the proper use of sound includes control of the two nostrils independent of each other,' and he goes on to say that 'all of us breathe differently through the nostrils according to our psychic, physical, and mental conditions, and according to the influences of the planets upon our psychic bodies.'[13]

Rama Prasad, who exhausted the subject of the yogic science of breath in *Nature's Finer Forces*, says that the left nostril is connected astrologically with Taurus, Cancer, Virgo, Scorpio, Capricorn, and Pisces, whereas the right nostril is connected with Aries, Gemini, Leo, Libra, Sagittarius, and Aquarius.[14] All the astrological planets affect the way we breathe through our nostrils – in effect, the astral body was so named originally because it was thought to be influenced by the planets – but the principal planet here is the closest – the Moon.

It seems appropriate somehow that the 'Moon Breath' should be affected by the Moon in the sky, and it does not surprise us that the Moon Breath is stronger during the two weeks of the Moon's waxing than during the two weeks of its waning.

Yogis say that the Moon Breath will be dominant at sunrise on the first day of the 'bright fortnight' and that the dominant nostril will change every two hours thereafter. The left nostril will again be dominant on the second and third days of the bright fortnight at sunrise, but on the fourth the pattern will reverse. On the fourth, fifth, and sixth days, the dominant nostril at sunrise will be the Sun Breath, changing again to the Moon Breath for three days beginning with the seventh day, and so on throughout the Lunar Month.

On the first day of the dark fortnight, when the Moon in the sky starts to wane, the Moon in the body will wane with it, and at sunrise on the first day of the dark fortnight we find that the Sun Breath is dominant.

All these astral influences can be counteracted by the state of the mind, which can be affected by other than astral influences. Thus, if the Sun Breath is not dominant at a certain time when the astrological influences indicate that it should be, some condition in your consciousness is interfering with this natural process. Ideally, this should never happen. To the extent that you do not follow the rhythms of nature, your mind is out of tune as it were, unless you are an adept, in which case you will direct your breath through the one nostril or the other without using your fingers, by will alone.

By will alone you may learn to direct the power of *prana* outside your body. Yogis have done some very odd experiments with this effect, directing their *prana* at a distance to some sick person for healing purposes; using it to 'charge' a bowl of water with energy before drinking it; even directing it into inanimate matter, to infuse it with life and consciousness. *Prana* is also connected with levitation, as I have said, and since *prana* can be made subservient to will, it is not surprising that a few people have learned to levitate by will alone.

One of these is Mikhail Drogzenovich, a Bulgarian farmer from the village of Stara Zagora. According to an East European newspaper, which is cited by Lynn Schroeder and Sheila Ostrander in *Psychic Discoveries Behind the Iron Curtain*, Mikhail's reputation as a levitator spread beyond his native village, and several scientists visited him at his farm to see a demonstration. He led them to a clearing in one of his fields, sat down, and closed his eyes in concentration. As his audience stared in amazement, he began to rise from the ground, floating slowly upward until he was suspended about four feet in the air. He remained there for ten minutes while his guests satisfied themselves that no trickery of any kind was being used, then floated to the ground again.

When asked how he did it, he said simply: 'I get there by will power.'[15]

In most cases the levitation is more partial than that. In *The Wisdom of the Mystic Masters* Joseph Weed tells of a woman he saw at an American fairground who had some ability to levitate. She stood on a scale first and showed her audience that she weighed fully 140 pounds. Then she stepped into what Weed described as 'a basket-like contrivance with a handle at the top' and invited members of the audience to lift her.

'I found to my surprise that I could lift her easily with one hand,' wrote Weed, 'yet on the scale her size indicated that the 140 pounds it recorded was correct. She could levitate to a small degree.

When Weed asked the woman how she did it, she could only say that her mother could do it and so could she. 'You can just make yourself feel lighter in here,' she said, putting her hand over her diaphragm. She had never been able to get off the ground, but she did feel very light at times, especially when she was a child, and when she fell, she never fell with a thud. 'I . . . always floated down gently, like a thistledown.'[16]

Something quite similar is cultivated in China by the masters of kung-fu, where it is called *ch'in kung*, or light walk. Michael Minick, who writes about this in *The Wisdom of Kung-Fu*, says that there are several training schemes. In one, the artist walks along the brim of a large jar filled with water. As he learns to maintain his balance, the jar is emptied, a little at a time. After years of work, he can walk easily along the rim of a completely empty jar, without tipping it over.

In another technique, the artist walks over very thin paper that is spread over loose sand. The object is to walk the distance of the paper without leaving footprints. Masters of ch'in kung, such as Yang lu-ch'an, are said to walk on freshly fallen snow without leaving a trace of their steps.[17]

In *The Psychic Side of Sports*, Michael Murphy and Rhen A. White suggest that in some sporting events 'the athlete is literally able to suspend himself in mid-air' for short periods of time. 'Basketball players and dancers especially seem to demonstrate this amazing ability.'[18]

Indeed, dancers sometimes do seem to demonstrate this ability, especially a Russian dancer named Nijinsky. Nandor Fodor insists that Nijinsky simply could not have executed some of the high leaps and slow descents that were so familiar to his audiences if he had not levitated to some degree. His development was undoubtedly unconscious – the result of innumerable attempts over a period of years to control his movements while in the air. But it proves the point none the less – that will alone can result in at least a partial ability to levitate.[19]

Now when mind is used to control *prana*, since mind is *prana*, we are in effect using our minds to control our minds. This produces an alteration in our state of consciousness, which means that levitation is never performed from a completely ordinary state of awareness.

To understand how this works, we shall have to take another page from the old yogic books. Yogis distinguish five states of consciousness. The first is ordinary waking consciousness, which is your state of consciousness right now as you are reading this book. The second is dream consciousness, or sleep with dreams. It is quite different from ordinary waking consciousness, and quite different also from the third state of consciousness, which is *dreamless* sleep. Beyond dreamless sleep is the 'cataleptic state,' and beyond that is what the Upanishads call 'undifferentiated consciousness of Bliss.'[20]

There are some variations on that system. Some authorities recognise only four states of consciousness, leaving out the so-called 'cataleptic state,' and there are occasionally some differences in terminology. The Maharishi Mahesh Yogi, for example, refers to 'undifferentiated consciousness of Bliss' as 'transcendental consciousness' (TC). In addition, he posits the existence of at least three additional states of consciousness beyond TC: cosmic consciousness, god consciousness, and unity consciousness. Some of Maharishi's former devotees say that to private students he reveals the existence of an even more advanced state of consciousness that he calls Brahman consciousness. But regarding the first four or five states, at least everybody is in broad agreement.[21]

In each of these states of awareness, man supposedly manifests in a different 'body.' Now I know that the idea of man having more than one body will seem strange, but it is part of the traditional theory of yoga, and some of these 'bodies' can be demonstrated to actually exist.

In the state of ordinary waking consciousness, man manifests in the physical body, called in Sanskrit the *sthula sharira*. In the dream state, he manifests in the 'subtle' or 'character' body – Western occultists would call it the astral body. In Sanskrit the name for this is *linga sharira*. It consists of three 'sheaths,' or subtle principles: the *jiva*, or vital force; the *manas*, or mind; and the *buddhi*, or understanding. Likewise, the dreamless sleep state is associated with the sheath of *jivatman*, the volitional body or causal body (*karana sharira*). In addition, each of these states of consciousness is characterised by different styles of breathing. One breathes differently in different states of awareness, as we have said, and that brings us to the real practical secret of *pranayama*.

Yogis say that everyone experiences all the states of awareness I have just mentioned every day, but that most people are unaware of their more profound experiences because to get to the state of pure awareness one must first pass through the state of unconsciousness, or deep sleep. By using *pranayama* to gradually slow down the breathing process, one can alter one's state of awareness at will, and thereby experience all the states at will and with full possession of one's conscious powers. This is not easy to do at first. When you approach the breathing rhythm associated with deep sleep you will probably start to doze off at first. But if you remember to sit in *asana*, and you practise assiduously, you will find that in time you can achieve the desired results.

Now here I have to issue one of my warnings again. *Pranayama*, as you will learn from experience, is the technique that certain fakirs in the East use to put themselves in a state of suspended animation. What they do is simply slow down the breathing and the heartbeat until they stop altogether. The person does not precisely 'die' because the process has been so gradual that there is no organic damage. By applying certain occult processes, the fakir's assistant can restore him to full consciousness, and, in the meantime, he will have had some extraordinary experiences on the Inner Planes. This is how such individuals as Tahra Bey have managed to be buried alive. But I must caution you not to try it yourself. This is a very advanced exercise and is under absolutely no circumstances ever performed without a knowledgeable person in attendance at all times to give medical assistance if needed. When I was in San Francisco in 1972, the newspapers were full of stories about a man in New Jersey who had been foolish enough to try the suspended animation experimentation alone. His diary indicated that he had been approaching it slowly over a period of some months as a means of acquiring 'astro-projection' (sic!), but there was nobody around to help him return to his physical body until it was too late. His trip to the Inner Planes was a one-way affair.

There is, of course, no danger if you use a little common sense. You cannot just slip accidentally into the state of suspended animation. And for our purposes nothing that extreme is necessary.

In the *Sivagama*, an ancient yogic book quoted by Rama Prasad in *Nature's Finer Forces*, some effort is made to tabulate the relative pranic conditions of different types of men and different states of awareness. In an ordinary man sitting quietly, the Human Aura, which is a manifestation of *prana*, surrounds the body at a distance of about twelve fingers. When he is speaking or eating, the distance increases to eighteen. When walking, it increases to twenty four; when running, to forty-two; when having sex, to sixty-five; and when sleeping, to one hundred.

These distances can be modified either by activity or by yoga. When one takes a deep breath, which is to say when one performs *Puraka*, the length diminishes by two fingers. Thus when the ordinary man takes a deep breath the 'length' of his *prana* diminishes from twelve to ten. The more the length diminishes the less ordinary a man he becomes.

In the *Sivagama* it is said that the man who is free from all desires has a 'length' of eleven fingers – one less than the 'ordinary' man. A person who is always pleasant and who has a well-developed sense of humour has a 'length' of ten fingers. A poet has a 'length' of nine fingers. A great orator has a 'length' of eight fingers. A seer, which is to say a person possessed of second sight, has a 'length' of seven fingers, and a levitator has a 'length,' of six fingers.[22]

As the 'length' diminishes still further, the results become more extraordinary. Thus a person with only five fingers has supernatural speed, with four one manifests the Eight Siddhis, with three the Nine Nidhis, and so forth. I realise that this is not a perfect system, but it can give you an idea where you stand in regard to levitation. If you are a poet or a budding Demosthenes you will have an easier time of it than a man who is merely pleasant. And if you have second sight you are almost there.

Now before I close this chapter I want to describe to you a very simple experiment that you can perform to prove to yourself the truth of some of the principles discussed here. I am not going to give you levitation exercises here, because I want to hold those for chapter 8. But I am going to give you an experiment that will prove to you the relationship between Mind and *Prana*.

This experiment is used in Aikido classes for this very purpose, yet it is so simple that anyone can succeed with it on the first try. It is called the 'unbending arm' experiment, and to do it you will need an assistant.

Ideally, your assistant should be a person of the same sex as you, of about the same height, and the same physical strength. You must stand facing your assistant and extend your right arm, so that your palm faces upward and your wrist rests on the other person's left shoulder. Now invite your assistant to try to bend your arm, using both his hands to do it. You will find that you have very poor leverage with your arm extended in this manner, and that your assistant can bend your arm quite easily, despite your efforts to keep the arm straight. Try this two or three times to prove to yourself that when you are in this position you simply do not have the strength to keep your arm straight if your assistant is trying to bend it. (If you can keep it straight, then you and your assistant are probably not evenly matched in strength – find another assistant!)

Once you have proved the point about the leverage, I want you to try again to keep your arm straight, only this time use *prana* instead of your muscular strength. Leave your right wrist resting on your assistant's shoulder, and relax your arm as much as you possibly can and still keep it in the desired position. Extend your fingers, close your eyes, and visualise a golden stream of *prana* flowing through your arm, through your fingers, and shooting through space into the visualization, and again ask your assistant to try to bend your arm. He will be altogether unable to do so, and yet you will not have to exert any effort to stop him. This is the kind of power that can be released using simple visualization techniques to control *prana*. Next, we are going to find out about some others.

Chapter Eight

SANYAMA

If *prana* is mind and mind is *prana*, then *prana* controls mind, and mind controls *prana*. That suggests that some of the benefits of pranayama might be attainable by nonmechanical means.

Yogis say that any movement of *prana*, however slight, results in a corresponding movement in the mind. That movement may be imperceptible, but it is there. And it is an impediment to yogic concentration.

That is the main reason why *pranayama* was developed – as an aid to concentration. Rather than attack the concentration problem frontally, by forcing the mind, yogis play little tricks on the mind, thereby achieving the same result much more effectively and with less effort.

Now when we do siddhis we do much the same thing. We do not try to force the siddhis to manifest themselves. We merely create the proper conditions and hold the desire in our minds that this or that siddhi should be made manifest.

In levitation, creating the proper conditions means doing *pranayama*, and doing *pranayama* means holding the breath.

What we want to do, then, is hold the breath, but without doing *pranayama*, and thereby concentrate the mind, but without using force. We need another trick, and the yogic trick that we shall use here is given in a yogic treatise translated by W. Y. Evans-Wentz in *Tibetan Yoga and Secret Doctrines*. I quote:

> Ordinarily the intellect is controlled by the senses. It is the sight which chiefly controlleth it.[1]

By arresting the senses, one arrests the mind, and by arresting the mind, one arrests the breath. There are two ways of arresting the senses, one internal and one external. We shall consider each of these in turn.

The internal method is called *Pratyahara*, which means 'sense withdrawal.' It is mentioned in *The Yoga Sutras* of Patanjali (pronounced Pah-*tah*-njelly, with emphasis on the second syllabic), and is one of the Eight Limbs of yoga.

It is also one of the most misunderstood techniques in all yogic occultism. Various authors tell us how to force out our senses, or force ourselves not to heed them, but that is absurd. Have you ever tried to shut out the noise of a freight train? Whenever you encounter a brute force technique in connection with yoga and the mind, you may be certain the author does not know enough about the techniques he is describing to teach. Brute force does not work with the mind and knowledgeable yogis do not use it.

Pratyahara is a condition, rather than a technique, that sets in after you have been meditating for some period of time. It can also result from *pranayama*. Says the *Siva Samhita*:

> When [the yogi] gets the power of holding breath for three hours, then certainly the wonderful state of *pratyahar* [sic] is reached without fail.[2]

I have found that no more than forty-five minutes is usually required, but there are variations from person to person, and the three hours mentioned in the *Siva Samhita* is certainly valid. Anyone who has been meditating *that* long is certainly in *Pratyahara*.

The way to find out is to sit in the full lotus on the floor and place an alarm clock on a low table, so that it is very close to one of your ears while you are meditating. Set the alarm for a time forty-five minutes to an hour later, then close your eyes and start doing *Japa*. Use whatever mantra you selected for yourself in chapter 4, and continue your meditation until you hear the alarm.

If you have entered *Pratyahara* by the time the alarm goes off, you may not hear it, or if you do, you will hear it the way you would if it had been put at the other end of a very long tunnel, four or five miles away. If you had not expected to hear the alarm when you started your meditation, your mind would have shut out the sound altogether.

I remember a group meditation session I attended in 1972. It was autumn, the leaves were on the ground, and after the group had been meditating for forty minutes or so, the caretakers outside the building we were using started gathering the leaves using petrol-powered vacuum cleaners. Now there are few things in the world that are noisier than a petrol-powered vacuum cleaner. An enraged dinosaur, maybe, or the tail-end of the Concorde at take-off time. Yet no one in the room heard them. It was not that we were trying to force the sound out of our minds. We were not aware that there was a sound to force out. We were in *Pratyahara*.

It is because of Pratyahara that you want to be certain you are sitting in a comfortable position whenever you start a long meditation. Your legs could go to sleep, and your back could be killing you, yet once you are in *Pratyahara* you will be dead to the things your body is telling you. I have emerged from *Pratyahara*, only to wish I had not. Some people enter the state so profoundly that they are able to endure terrible pain without suffering. In fact, there are stories of great yogis who have faced their own deaths in just that way.

To understand just how this is possible, or why it matters, I shall have to digress for a moment and say something about the structure of the mind. Swami Vivekananda gives the classical yogic explanation in his article on 'Pranayama':

The mind is like an ocean in which a wave arises, but although the man sees the wave, he does not know how the wave came there, whence its birth, or whither it melts down again; he cannot trace it any further. But when 'the perception becomes finer, we can trace this wave long, long before it comes to the surface; and we will be able to trace it for a long distance after it has disappeared.[3]

The Maharishi Mahesh Yogi says much the same thing in *The Science of Being and Art of Living* except that he likens thoughts to bubbles, rather than waves.

> A thought starts from the deepest levels of consciousness, travels through the whole depth of the ocean of mind, and finally appears as a conscious thought on the surface. Thus we find that every thought stirs the whole range of the depth of consciousness, but that it is consciously appreciated only when it has come to the *conscious* level.[4]

In meditation we begin with a thought, and try to plunge into the ocean of the mind, staying with our thought and experiencing it at more and more profound levels until we go beyond the point at which thought originates. Since sense-impressions can only be appreciated at the conscious level, or at the surface of the ocean of the mind, the deeper we go into the ocean of mind, the deeper we go into *Pratyahara*.

This has certain advantages, because the mind is a lot like a literal ocean. However turbulent the ocean may be on the surface, the depths below are always peaceful and still. And so it is with the mind. By diving into the ocean of mind during meditation one can experience these deeper and quieter levels and bring some of this quietness back to the surface.

Now to do this we start with a thought that is nonintellectual. We want to think the thought, but we want to think it without arousing the brain to any greater level of activity. The phrase 'nonintellectual' thought may seem like a semantic self-contradiction, but it is not really, because a thought does not have to be something out of Plato or Aristotle. You can think almost anything. And in meditation we think the mantras.

A mantra is a thought that is almost totally devoid of intellectual content. If we thought *about* the mantra we could make it intellectual. But if we simply think the mantra itself there is no intellectual activity taking place. That allows the brain to function at quieter levels of lesser activity, and as this happens and we continue thinking the mantra we eventually reach the point at which thought originates. At this point the mantra disappears. We have transcended thought itself.

This is significant because as Maharishi himself points out: "All the psychic powers belong naturally to the field of the Being," meaning the pure consciousness at which thought has been transcended. 'If there could be a way to directly come in contact and be familiar with the field of the Being, then all the psychic powers and all the powers of nature belonging to the almighty eternal Being will be available.'⁵

Pratyahara therefore becomes a sign that we are approaching the state of pure awareness at which the psychic powers become available. Later on I shall tell you how to make use of that fact.

The other form of sense restraint that I mentioned is *Dharana* – concentration. *Dharana* can be performed on four different types of objects: external objects, internal objects, qualities, and mental concepts, but the last three are quite difficult to master. Therefore, I have called *Dharana* an external technique.

Dharana simply means fixing the senses on some selected object and not allowing them to wander therefrom. *Dharana* can be done with any of the five senses, but since sight is said in yoga to be chief among the senses, *Dharana* usually means visual concentration.

In Tibet, occultists often perform *Dharana* on a stick or a wooden ball, whereas in India the object of choice is a candle flame. But I am going to suggest that you start out with your own image in a mirror, for two reasons: this *Dharana* is just as effective as the others, and it leads quickly to one of the siddhis – remembrance of past incarnations.

You will need a mirror that measures about eight inches by four inches, with the plainest frame you can find (or no frame at all, if you are not averse to dismantling it), and a plain glass surface. Do not use any of the very ornate mirrors that are available with gold decorations on the glass, and do not use a mirror that is too large.

Remember, the object of this exercise is visual concentration. Anything that will distract your eye while you are doing the exercise must be avoided.

Once you have selected your mirror, put it on a table if you are sitting in a chair, or on the floor, if you are sitting on the floor, and put something behind it to support it. If you are sitting on the floor in the full lotus you might want to lean the mirror against one of the walls of your meditation room. Position it so that you can see your face in it without straining your neck, and position yourself no more than three feet away from it, so that you can perform your *Dharana* without eyestrain.

Now subdue the lights. If you are doing the exercise at night, turn off any electric lights that you may have in the room, and place a single candle close enough to the mirror that you have sufficient illumination, far enough away that you are not distracted. If it is daytime, close your curtains so that you allow only just enough indirect sunlight into the room that you can see clearly, but not enough that the room is brilliantly lit. Above all, avoid situating yourself so that the sun or any other source of illumination shines in your face while you are doing the experiment.

Once you have all *that* straightened out, sit comfortably before the mirror, adjust the mirror so that you can see your entire face in it, and look yourself in the right eye. You will find that your eyes make the best objects for this kind of concentration. It makes no difference whether you use your right eye or your left eye, but you will have better results concentrating on your eye than you would on your nose or mouth or hair.

Fix your gaze on your right eye and keep it there. If you blink, you will have broken concentration. If you let your eyes wander, ever so slightly, you will have broken your concentration. To achieve success you are going to have to concentrate perfectly, and maintain that concentration for a half hour or more.

You will not be able to do it at first, but with practice it will come easily. After three or four tries you should begin to get some results.

One thing that may happen is that the whole room may seem to go dark for just a moment. This is a sign of progress; when it happens, just ignore it and continue your concentration. You may also begin to see a golden radiance emanating from your face. This is a very auspicious sign. But do not let these experiences distract you. Remember, if you let your eyes wander or if you blink you will have lost everything you have gained and you will have to start over again.

At some point you may begin to see that some portion of your face has changed. It will only be one or two features at first. You may feel that your nose has changed shape or that a portion of your face has been obscured by a picture of another face. You may also see the feature of this second face emerging from the golden radiance that will appear. In time, if you persevere, a completely different face may emerge in the mirror. You will be able to see it quite clearly, and when you do, make note: this is the way you appeared in a previous incarnation.

I have been told that the first face to appear is either the face of your most dominant past personality, or else the face of your most recent incarnation. When you have acquired the ability to see the faces clearly, ask yourself who this person was, when and where he lived, and what his life means to you now. You may find the answers surprising.

In time you will be able to get other faces, which represent more remote personalities. In this manner, I have been able to discover that I have died at the hands of the Spanish Inquisition, that I spent a lifetime as a wealthy, but other-worldly merchant in Japan, and that I ended my last lifetime as a European Jew in one of Hitler's concentration camps. Not all of your past-life experiences will have been pleasant, but they will all be interesting. And this little experiment, which is quite easy for most people to master, will give you a good, practical 'feel' for the more difficult *Dharanas* to follow. If you do an open-eye *Dharana* on something other than your face, you may have a peculiar experience that is mentioned in *The Yoga Sutras*, in which you feel that you are blending, or merging, with the object of your concentration.

Dr. A. J. Deikman, of the University of Colorado Medical School, actually tried some of Patanjali's methods on some experimental subjects; According to his report in *The Journal of Nervous and Mental Disease*, the subjects were asked to sit about ten feet from an ordinary brown end table, on which he had placed a blue vase. His subjects were asked to look at the vase, but not to study or analyse it. The sessions started out lasting ten minutes, then were gradually extended to thirty minutes' duration.

Dr. Deikman found that 'very striking changes in the perception of the self and of the object were possible' and that after thirty to forty sessions 'the beginnings of breakdown of the self-object distinction' were noticed.[6] In the words of one of his subjects, a thirty-eight year old psychiatric nurse:

> It was as though we were together, you know, instead of being a table and a vase and me, my body and the chair, it was all dissolved into a bundle of something which had . . . a great deal of energy to it but which doesn't form into anything but it only feels like a force.[7]

Aleister Crowley claimed in his *Confessions* that this experience could come with 'explosive violence' and that the meditator's mind could be so zapped that he couldn't even remember it. Most people do remember it, though.[8]

According to a Mr. David Birdsell of Connecticut – quoted by John Weldon and Zola Levitt in *The Transcendental Explosion* – 'it is not uncommon for advanced (TM) meditators to have experiences of objects and people psychically merging with them.'[9]

Colin Bennett described something of the sort in his book *Practical Time Travel*, published by The Aquarian Press (1980). He is interested in crystal gazing, which is, after all, an open-eyed *Dharana*, and which leads to what he calls the 'mystic phenomenon of the crystal absorbing the gazer.'[10]

> The sphere appears to swell, so that its face draws nearer and nearer until the gazer finds himself enveloped in it. The culminating point of this experience is always sudden, and its duration may be quite short. While it lasts the percipient not merely sees a past event in miniature upon the crystal's face, but becomes one with it.[11]

Another story of the type comes from Max Long's *Recovering the Ancient Magic*, also cited by Bennett. Long claims to have met a fire-eater on an American fairground who could play the flame of a blowtorch on his exposed tongue without the benefit of protective chemicals. His explanation was that years before he had studied under a magician, who encouraged him to spend several hours a day effectively performing open-eyed Dharana on a 'sacred butter lamp.' One day the flames from the lamp appeared to leap out and engulf his entire body for a moment, and after that he felt that he had become one with Fire and under its protection.[12]

That this could happen – that the yogi could feel that he had become one with whatever he uses for concentration – suggests that his consciousness does not remain static while he is doing *Dharana*. In other words, the yogi is not merely arresting his gaze; he is producing profound and even startling alterations in his state of awareness.

These alterations are the basis for Siddhi performance. Yogis say that there is in fact a definite cycle of conscious-alterations that takes place, and when the yogi completes his cycle he is said to have done *Sanyama*.

Sanyama is a Sanskrit word, like all the other words we have used, and, like the others, it comes from Patanjali's *Yoga Sutras*. It literally means 'going together' because in *Sanyama* three different phases of consciousness 'go together.' These are: *Dharana*, *Dhyana*, and *Samadhi*.

Let us use the mirror experiment to explain how this works. When you first started concentrating on your right eye, you were aware of the eye, and you were aware of yourself, but you were also aware of everything else in the room. You were aware that you were looking in a mirror, that you were sitting on the floor, that you were in such and such a place, and so on. This is *Dharana*. It is concentration, but it is not yogically perfect concentration.

If you persisted in your concentration, it eventually deepened, so that you excluded everything from your awareness except yourself and your image in the mirror. This is *Dhyana*. Then, if you persisted still further, your concentration would have deepened to the point that you lost awareness even of yourself. There remained only the object.

This last stage is called *Samadhi*, and it is in this stage that the mystic union of the perceiver and perceived takes place. Having lost awareness of himself, the yogi feels that he literally becomes whatever he is concentrating on.

'The passage from "concentration" (*Dharana*) to "meditation" (*Dhyana*) requires no new technique,' writes Mircea Eliade. 'Similarly, no supplementary yogic exercise is needed to realise *Samadhi* once the yogi has succeeded in "concentrating" and "meditating."'[13]

There is an ancient formula according to which one *Dharana* requires twelve seconds of unbroken concentration. One *Dhyana* is twelve *Dharanas*, and one *Samadhi* is twelve *Dhyanas*. Thus to reach *Samadhi* requires twelve times twelve times twelve seconds, or 1728 seconds, or 28.8 minutes. I have always felt that these kinds of formulas are a little artificial, but the times are not too far off. It will take you about half an hour to reach *Samadhi* at first. But the Adepts are said to reach it instantly.

Now in the more advanced siddhis, such as levitation, we do not use an external object for Sanyama. We use some internal object, and often a visualised image. You are not likely to experience the definite stages of *Dhrana*, *Dhyana*, and *Samadhi* in the same perceptual fashion as you will when you are using an external object. And so we define the stages differently.

Recall for a moment the metaphor of the 'ocean of the mind.' As we proceed from the top of the ocean – the surface level of awareness – to the bottom, which represents the state of pure consciousness, we pass through certain intermediate levels of consciousness. Most occult writers speak of these levels in a rather nebulous fashion, but some try to quantify them. Some schools maintain that there are seven levels of consciousness; others that there are twelve. But for our purpose, we say that there are three. The ocean has a surface, a middle, and a floor. A journey has a beginning, a middle, and an end. And *Sanyama* has *Dharana*, *Dhyana*, and *Samadhi*.

Dharana is therefore the state in which you are concentrating, but essentially functioning at the surface level of your mind. As your concentration deepens, you dive beneath the surface. You are in *Dhyana*. Then, when you reach the stage of pure awareness, you have reached *Samadhi*.

According to Professor Orme-Johnson, this is the interpretation of *Sanyama* that is used in the TM-Sidhi Programme. Mantra meditation can then be seen as a form of *Sanyama* on the mantra, and the specific benefits accruing therefrom as the 'siddhis' that this form of *Sanyama* confers.[14]

Now there are two types of siddhis that are acquired through *Sanyama*: Knowledge Siddhis and Power Siddhis. The reincarnation experiment with the mirror is an example of the first class of siddhis. Levitation is an example of the second.

All the Power Siddhis are based on the same esoteric principle: that when the mystic union between the perceiver and the perceived takes place and the *Samadhi* results, the yogi acquires extraordinary power over the objects of his attention.

In the fire *Sanyama* that I described earlier, the fire-eater that Max Long discovered acquired through *Sanyama* on his butter lamp an unusual degree of mastery over fire. By becoming one with fire in *Samadhi* he was able to direct its powers and potencies in a way that would be impossible for an ordinary man. As Evans-Wentz says of the yogi: 'He must be able to make his body immune to each of the elements, including fire, as suggested in the fire-walking ceremony, and to the law of gravitation, as in levitation.'[15] The only difference is that in levitation we use a different object for *Sanyama* than fire. We do *Sanyama* on *prana*.

This makes sense because, as I have said, levitation involves the use of *prana*, and it would therefore be *prana* that we would seek to arouse and master. But not just *any prana*.

In past chapters I have always spoken of *prana* as a single power or energy in the universe, and in the universe it is singular. But inside the human body we say that there are ten *pranas*, or, more precisely, that there are ten *Vayus*, or 'airs.' Five of these have to do with the outer body and serve purely physical functions. The other five have to do with the inner (astral) body, and are used in the occult sciences.

The five *Vayus* of the outer body are *Naga*, *Kurma*, *Krikara*, *Devadatta*, and *Dhananjaya*. *Naga* is associated with eructation, and gives rise to consciousness. *Kurma* opens the eyes and causes vision. *Krikara* is involved during sneezing, and causes hunger and thirst. *Devadatta* is involved in yawning. And *Dhananjaya* is involved in hiccoughing and the production of sound. According to the *Gheranda Samhita*, *Dhananjaya* 'pervades the whole gross body and does not leave it even after death.'[16]

The five *Vayus* of the inner body are *Prana*, *Apana*, *Samana*, *Udana*, and *Vyana*. These *Vayus* have specific esoteric functions, in addition to their physical activities, and one of them, the *Udana,* is specifically involved in levitation.

The *Udana* is situated physically in the throat, and is involved physically in swallowing and in the movements of chyle through the digestive system. It is also involved in putting you to sleep. According to Vachaspati, *Udana* manifests from the forepart of the nose to the top of the head, thereby serving as an astral connecting link between the three highest chakras in the human system: the *Visuddhi* in the throat, the *Ajna* between the eyebrows, and the *Sahasrara* at the top of the head. Alice Bailey says that the *Udana* 'has a special relationship to the brain, the nose, and the eyes, and, when properly controlled, produces the coordination of the vital airs and their correct handling.'[17] The word *Udana* derives from the Sanskrit root *ut*, which means 'to carry upward.'

It is this quality of carrying upward that makes the *Udana* valuable in levitation. In Book 3, *Sutra* number thirty-eight of Patanjali's *Yoga Sutras*, we read: 'By mastery of the *Udana*, [the yogi acquires] ascension and non-contract with water, thorns, mire, etc.'

I. K. Taimni interprets this as meaning that '*Udana* is obviously connected with the gravitational pull of the earth on the body, and by controlling this particular *prana* it is possible to neutralise this pull.'[18] Alice Bailey says of *Udana* that 'levitation, the power to walk on water, and the ability to withstand the gravitational pull of the earth is its lowest and least important significance.'[19]

Vachaspati, one of Patanjali's early commentators, says that 'ascension . . . takes place by the path which has its beginning in the flame [the *Archiradi*, northern path] after death. Having mastered that path, he [the yogi] ascends by that path.'[20] Some authorities interpret this to mean that nobody can master the *Udana* completely unless he is a very advanced yogi and near death. Lesser students can try, though, and Vachaspati tells us precisely how to proceed. '*Udana*,' he says, 'is mastered by the performance of *Sanyama* thereupon.'[21]

Sit on the floor, get into the full lotus, close your eyes, and start your mantra. When you feel that you have introverted your consciousness, visualise a very thin white line, the thickness of a human hair, extending from the region of your throat to the forepart of your nose, then to the space between your eyebrows, and finally to the top of your head. In doing this visualization, you want to imagine this white line as being within your body, and you want to make your visualization so vivid that you can actually see it. You want to feel that if it were outside your body, where it would be accessible, you could reach out and touch it, so vivid should your mental image be.

Once you have the line firmly in your mind and you can see it, try to become aware of the *Udana* that it represents. Try to feel the energy coursing through the upper part of your body, and try especially to feel the upward direction of this energy. You will find this easier than the visualization. The first few times, you may feel a tingling sensation in the area of the *Udana*, later, you may feel some pressure as the energy becomes stronger. And later still, you will feel a very definite, pulsating, upward current of energy that manifests most strongly in the upper part of your head, between the area between your eyebrows and the area of the top of your head.

Now you want to try to increase the *Udana's* power. Imagine that your white line is starting to swell. Imagine that it is growing larger, and that the energy that it represents is growing as well, becoming more and more powerful, until its power to carry upward becomes so immense that it can literally carry your body upward, and suspend you above water, thorns, and mire. You will find this an exhilarating meditation to perform, even before you begin to get objective results.

Now when you do this meditation, I want you to remember that the *Udana* you are visualizing in your head and neck is not something you are merely imagining. *Udana* may not appear in any of the charts produced by Western physiologists, but it is quite real, nonetheless, and if you persist in your visualization, you will acquire the ability to actually see, not just a visualised image, but the *Udana* itself.

The siddhi involved here is the ability to see things that are hidden from view, and the technical principles are the same as those involved in the astral projection exercises of chapter 3. You will recall that you visualised the room surrounding you and tried to 'see' the room, even though you had your eyes closed. In this case, you will visualise the *Udana* and try to 'see' it inside your body, even though it is something that ordinarily you could not see even if your eyes were not closed. This is the way psychic abilities are developed, by holding in the mind the desire and the will to do something that ordinarily cannot be done. Once you acquire the ability to actually see the *Udana*, you will be doing *Sanyama* on the *Udana* itself, rather than a visualised image, and your technique will become more powerful.

Sanyama is performed on all the five *Vayus* in the same way – by visualizing that *Vayu* within the human body, by directing the attention to that part of the body for an extended period of time, and by holding in mind the desire that that particular *Vayu* come under conscious control. I have not the space in this book to go into all the potencies of all the five *Vayus*, but I do want to leave you with at least the knowledge of where they are located within the human system and where their particular areas of manifestation are. Remember, each of the five *Vayus* has a seat within the body, defined by such texts as the *Siva Samhita*, and each of the five *Vayus* also has a particular area of manifestation, which is given by Vyasa in his commentary on Patanjali's *Yoga Sutras*. This is shown in the following table:

Vayu	Seat	Area of Manifestation
Apana	Rectal-genital area	Bottom of feet to solar plexus
Vyana	None	All over body
Samana	Solar plexus	Solar plexus to heart
Prana	Heart	Heart to forepart of nose
Udana	Throat	Forepart of nose to top of head

In addition to the *Udana Sanyama*, Patanjali gives us another levitation technique, which is described in *Sutra* number forty-two. He says: 'By *Sanyama* on the relationship between the body and the *Akasa* and on the lightness of such things as cotton down, the yogi acquires passage through the sky.'

This has been mistakenly interpreted as a teleportation technique, or as an astral projection technique. But it is a levitation technique. And it is a particularly interesting levitation technique because it is the one used by the Maharishi Mahesh Yogi in the TM-Sidhi Programme. It is therefore the levitation technique that has been used by more people than any other. And that may be an important point to some prospective levitators.

There is a frank admission of this in a book called *An Invitation to Enlightenment*, which was published by the Maharishi International University in Fairfield, Iowa. According to this booklet, 'the TM-Sidhi abilities are performances of higher states of consciousness described in the yoga system of Patanjali,' and the particular ability called 'passage through the sky' is defined as 'reorientation of the physiology and some tendency to levitate.'[22] The booklet then gives a brief synopsis of a paper by Dr. David Orme-Johnson and his colleagues, entitled 'Higher States of Consciousness: EEG Coherence, Creativity, and Experiences of the Sidhis' in which the same admission is made.[23]

That being the case, it might not be inappropriate to review some of Maharishi's theories about these higher states of consciousness before we go any further.

As I pointed out earlier, Maharishi distinguishes at least seven, and possibly eight, distinct states of awareness. The lowest is ordinary waking consciousness, followed by dream consciousness and sleep consciousness, which for most people is un-consciousness. But beyond those three he adds a fourth, which he calls *transcendental consciousness*, TC for short. It is not a new discovery, and he admits as much in his commentary, *On the Bhagavad-Gita*, but Maharishi gives an old idea a new twist. Transcendental consciousness as he calls it is *kshanika-samadhi*, or temporary *Samadhi*. It is the third stage of *Sanyama*, and, so that there is no doubt of the connection, he tells us that 'transcendental meditation' – his meditation technique, which is actually just *Japa*, or mantra chanting – 'belongs to the sphere of *dhyana*.[24] TM is therefore a form of *Sanyama*, as I pointed out earlier, and it is through the practice of TM that Maharishi proposes to manifest the siddhis.

Traditionally, one has achieved *samadhi* – the third stage of *Sanyama* – through prolonged concentration on the objects prescribed by this or that Sutra. But Maharishi, if I understand him correctly, proposes that we first achieve *samadhi* and *then* perform the siddhi. The siddhis then become an indicator of our success in reaching *samadhi*. And there is another benefit as well.

As Maharishi explains it, the supreme object of yoga is to gradually transform *kshanika*, or temporary, *samadhi* into *nitya*, or permanent, *samadhi*. This is done by experiencing *kshanika samadhi* every day through meditation so that the state carries over into activity as it were. Once this happens, one has attained what Maharishi chooses to call cosmic consciousness, or CC – the fifth state of consciousness, beyond transcendental consciousness. There is, then, a duality of awareness if you will, with the transcendental state of awareness coexisting with ordinary waking consciousness, and, when one sleeps, with the other two states of awareness that ordinary people experience. Some long-term meditators report that they have the feeling of 'witnessing sleep,' which means in effect that while their body is asleep their mind is awake. They are simultaneously in the sleep state and the transcendental state of consciousness.[25]

When this happens, one is able to act from the state of transcendental consciousness, and that is precisely what one does when performing one of the siddhis. That is why Maharishi refers to the siddhis as 'transcendental consciousness in action.' And that is also why the siddhis are taught. Because by deliberately performing the siddhis, one deliberately acts from the state of transcendental awareness. And to the extent one acts from the state of transcendental awareness, one is moving toward the state of *nitya-samadhi* – cosmic consciousness – in which one acts from TC all the time.

Now for the technique. There are several different interpretations of the 'passage through the sky' Sutra that are really just different levels of interpretation. I believe it is important that the would-be levitator understands the Sutra from all of these levels, and to that end I propose to discuss it rather deeply.

Some translators prefer to render the word *Akasa* 'space,' so that the Sanskrit *kayakasayoh* becomes 'body and space' and the phrase *cakasagamanam* becomes 'passage through space.' This is a perfectly acceptable alternative translation, and when we use it the Sutra reads: 'By Sanyama on the relationship between the body and *space* and on the lightness of such things as cotton down, the yogi acquires passage through *space*.'

In the light of the general theory underlying Patanjali's *Yoga Sutras*, the meaning now becomes clear. Through *Sanyama* one achieves mastery over the object thereof. Therefore, by doing *Sanyama* on the relationship between the body and space, one acquires mastery of that relationship – thus passage through space. This is confirmed by Vyasa in his commentary on Patanjali, thus:

> Wherever there is the body, there is space (*Akasa*), because space (*Akasa*) makes way for the body. They have relationship to each other because the body is pervaded by space. Through *Sanyama* on this relationship, and on gaining the lightness of things such as cotton, etc., on down to the atom, the yogi becomes light himself. Thence he gains the power of walking on water with his feet, then walking on a spider's webs, and finally walking on rays of light. Thereafter, he walks through space at will.

In a Buddhist magical text that is translated by Conze in his *Buddhist Scripture*, we are told that 'a sensation of ease and lightness' comes over the yogi when he performs this meditation. 'The sensation should be regarded as one of lightness,' says the text, 'because it is free from the (five) Hindrances, and from other states hostile to trance, such as discursive thinking, and so on. As soon as this sensation has come over the monk, his physical body becomes as light as a tuft of cotton wool. And so he goes to the Brahmaworld with his visible body as light as a tuft of cotton-down blown along by the wind.'[26]

Once this lightness has been attained, the text recommends that one either use the 'earth-device' or else will that a magical wind arise and blow one to the desired destination. 'The desire to move along is the decisive factor.'

Now the 'earth-device' is merely a visualization, in which you imagine that a certain area of space has become solid, so that you can walk on it. Obviously, the earth-device is useless unless you have first acquired the sense of lightness. And the sense of lightness is useless unless you have translated it into physical terms, that is, unless the sense of lightness is more than just a sense.

As I pointed out in chapter 4, a sense of lightness is likely to come over you as you are meditating, but, in this case, we produce the sense deliberately. As Vyasa says, we perform *Sanyama* on the relationship between the body and space, which is to say that we meditate until we attain the state of *samadhi*, or pure awareness, then meditate on the fact that the body is pervaded by space. As the *Siva Samhita* says: 'space pervades the five false states of matter but does not mix with them.'[27] As you imagine your body becoming pervaded with space, you will feel a gradual feeling of lightness coming over you. This is the lightness of which the Sutra speaks. If you feel it, that is your assurance that you are performing the siddhi correctly.

Those who have actually managed to leave the ground have described the experience in various ways. One meditator, quoted in *New Realities*, likens the experience to 'a blast of energy through the body and a sensation of incredible lightness.'[28] Another levitator speaks of feeling 'a tremendous amount of energy go through me' and having a vision of his chest and spine as a 'white light.'[29] Joseph Weed, who interviewed a number of levitators years ago, notes that 'those who have succeeded explain that it is not too difficult to repeat once achieved, not too unlike learning to swim.'[30]

One of the best descriptions of the levitation experience I have encountered appeared in Hugo Muensterberg's *Psychotherapy*. It comes from a lady who experienced it quite spontaneously, during an illness, after a visit from a faith healer.

I suddenly had a sensation of being lifted up or rising slowly and becoming lighter in body. *A rush of power that I have no way of describing to you* filled me. I seemed to be a tremendous dynamo in the air several inches above the ground and still ascending, when I noticed everything around me becoming prismatic and more or less translucent. I could have walked on water without sinking . . . Matter seemed to be disintegrating and dissolving around me. I remained in this state for about three hours, my consciousness seeming to have reached almost cosmic greatness . . . At the end of the day, towards twilight, the condition left me, and like the sudden dropping of a weight, I struck the ground, the same dull, ordinary person of everyday experience, but with the vast difference of perfect health, radiant and lasting to the present writing.[31]

Notice the common elements in every case: lightness of body, tremendous energy, etc. Professor Orme-Johnson and his colleagues at the Maharishi European Research University in Seelisberg, Switzerland have studied many such experiences and have arranged the different elements into a hierarchy of different levels. Thus, if you have experience number one, but not two to seven, you are at the beginning of your quest, whereas if you have experience number four you are quite advanced. Professor Orme-Johnson's list pertains specifically to TM levitators, but anyone working with these experiments is likely to have some of the same results:

(1) An awareness that the body is pervaded by space;

(2) A sense of lightness;

(3) An upward current of energy (as we noted earlier with the *Udana Sanyama*);

(4) Trembling and fast breathing (as noted with certain *pranayamas*);

(5) Hopping;

(6) Hopping with a sense of control and increased lightness;

(7) Hovering for a few seconds.[32]

Almost all of these categories of experiences have been noted in previous chapters, but not necessarily in a specific order. Notice that there is some overlap between one technique and another. Lightness, or as it is technically known in yoga, *Laghima*, has been noted in connection with meditation. Trembling and hopping have been noted in connection with *pranayama*. There is a very good reason for this, and to explain what that reason is, I want to penetrate deeper into the meaning of this Sutra. As I said earlier, there are several levels of interpretation of this Sutra. We have just examined the superficial levels.

I have pointed out that the Sanskrit *cakasagamanam* may be translated 'passage through the sky,' and that it may also be translated 'passage through space.' These two translations give us two different levels of meaning, and if we adopt a third, we have a still more profound level. Let us translate *cakasagamanam* 'passage through the *Akasa* and, for the sake of consistency, let us translate *kayakasayoh* as 'the body and *Akasa*. The Sutra now becomes: 'By *Sanyama* on the relationship between the body and *Akasa* and on the lightness of such things as cotton down, the yogi acquires passage through the *Akasa*.'

This may seem like a superficial change, but it is not really. There is much more to this Sutra than just passage through space because there is much more to the *Akasa* than just space.

According to the Vaisheshika system of Hindu philosophy, *Akasa* is one of the five *Tattwas*, or as the *Siva Samhita* would have it, one of the five 'false states' of matter. It corresponds in Greek philosophy to the Quintessence, the fifth essence that Aristotle added to the four proposed by Empedocles. In Theosophical terminology, it would be the fifth state of matter. The lower four *Tattwas* – *Prithivi*, *Apas*, *Tejas*, and *Vayu* – would be the first four states in Theosophy, or the Earth, Water, Fire, and Air Elements respectively.

Thus *Prithivi* represents the solid state, *Apas* represents the liquid state, *Tejas* represents the fiery state, and *Vayu* represents the gaseous state. *Akasa* then becomes ether, the fifth state of matter that is a thousand times rarer than the rarest gas.

The five *Tattwas* also correspond to the five *Indriyas,* or the subtle bases of the five senses. Thus *Prithivi* corresponds to smell, *Apas* to taste, *Tejas* to sight, *Vayu* to touch, and *Akasa* to sound. In addition, each of the *Tattwas* is said to have its seat in the human body at one of the five other chakras, thus:

Chakra	Location	Tattwa	Element
Muladhara	Base of spine	Prithivi	Earth
Svadisthana	Genital area	Apas	Water
Manipura	Solar plexus	Tejas	Fire
Anahat	Heart	Vayu	Air
Visuddha	Throat	Akasa	Quintessence
Ajna	Between eyebrows	—	—
Sahasrara	Top of head	—	—

The two highest chakras, the *Ajna* and the *Sahasrara*, correspond to what in Theosophy would be considered the sixth and seventh states of matter. They have names, but are not considered to be *Tattwas*, which is why they are not given here.

Now in the *Yogatattva Upanishad*, each of the five *Tattwas* is also said to have a specific area of manifestation in the body, in addition to its seat. Thus when one performs *Sanyama* on the *Akasa*, according to this system, one concentrates on a particular area of the body in which the *Akasa* manifests itself, and one mentally repeats a 'seed syllable' that is specific to the *Akasa*. In this system the phrase 'the relationship between the body and the *Akasa*' takes on a different meaning than in Vyasa's commentary. The body and the *Akasa* are related not because the body is pervaded by space, but because the *Akasa* is seated in a specific area in the body and because it has a certain specific area of manifestation. I am going to give all the areas of manifestation for all the *Tattwas* here because this ties in directly with some earlier statements I have made about the five *Vayus*:

Tattwa	Seed Syllable	Area of Manifestation
Prithivi	lam	Bottom of feet to knees
Apas	vam	Knees to rectal area
Tejas	ram	Rectal area to heart
Vayu	yam	Heart to mid-eyebrows
Akasa	ham	Mid-eyebrows to top of head

Notice that *Prithivi* has the same seat in the body and approximately the same area of manifestation as the *Apana Vayu*. Notice also that there is a correspondence between the *Samana Vayu* and the *Tejas Tattwa*. Notice that there is a correspondence between the *Prana Vayu* and the *Vayu Tattwa*. And notice most of all that there is a correspondence between the *Udana Prana* and the *Akasa*. Both the *Udana* and the *Akasa* are seated in the throat. And both the *Udana* and the *Akasa* manifest from the nose to the top of the head. This is a correspondence that is hinted at by Vyasa, but is never explicitly pointed out in any of the texts. Yet it is quite interesting to occultists because it shows that the *Udana Sanyama* and the *Akasa Sanyama* are almost the same *Sanyama*. That is why they produce the same results. By meditating on the one principle we affect the other.

As with other *Sanyamas*, your success in doing the *Akasa Sanyama* will depend on how well you attain the state of *Samadhi* – the third stage of *Sanyama*. This holds true whether you use the method outlined by Vyasa or that outlined in the *Yogatattva Upanishad*. To make it easier to get to *Samadhi*, we perform *Japa* as part of the technique, but we do not use the mantra selected in chapter 4. This time you should use a traditional mantra. There are five of these, or one for each of the five *Tattwas*, and the one for *Akasa* is 'ham.'

When you pronounce 'ham' to yourself, pronounce it *mentally*, and say it so that the 'ha' sound is very short, with the 'mmm' sound drawn out slightly. You may want to do fifteen or twenty minutes of *Japa* using the 'ham' as a mantra before even attempting the Sanyama itself. If you settle on Vyas's method, you have all the technique you need at this point. But if you decide you want to work with the method from the *Yogatattva Upanishad*, you will want to add a visualization. There are five of these visualizations, which consist of a colour and a shape for each of the five *Tattwas*. *Prithivi* is yellow and square. *Apas* is white, like the Moon, and half-circular. *Tejas* is red like fire and triangular, with the apex pointing upward. On *Vayu* and *Akasa*, though, there are differences of opinion from one text to the next.

In *The Gheranda Samhita*, the colour of *Akasa* is given as the colour of pure sea water, but in Rama Prasad's book, *Nature's Finer Forces*, *Akasa* is said to have the colour of darkness, 'foreshadowing all colours.'[33] *The Gheranda Samhita* does not give a form, but Rama Prasad says that *Akasa* is 'formless.'[34] Initiates of the Golden Dawn Order visualised it as a black oval. In any event, it should be imagined as seated in the throat and manifesting from the nose to the top of the head.

In the *Yogatattva Upanishad* we are told that *Sanyama* on any of the lower four *Tattwas* leads to harmlessness. That is, if you master *Prithivi* through *Sanyama* on it, you need not fear the Earth Element. If you master *Tejas*, you need not fear Fire. The fairground fire-eater mentioned by Max Long in *Recovering the Ancient Magic* would appear to have proved this. Likewise, *Sanyama* on *Vayu* leads to having nothing to fear from the atmosphere, and *Sanyama* on *Akasa* leads to 'movement through space.'[35] *The Gheranda Samhita* agrees in substance, but disagrees on the *Vayu* and *Akasa Sanyamas*. *Vayu Sanyama*, according to this text, leads to 'walking in air,' whereas *Akasa Sanyama* 'opens the gates of emancipation.'[36] We are to visualise the *Vayu Tattwa* as a sphere, full of '*Sattva* quality,' boiling and churning with a smoke-coloured energy. Maintain this visualization for five *ghatikas* – about two and a half hours – and the desired results are sure to come – so says *The Gheranda Samhita*.

In *Nature's Finer Forms*, Rama Prasad quotes the *Sivagama* as advising us to 'meditate on the Vayu, with PAM as the algebraical symbol, as being spherical, sky-blue, and giving the power of going into space, and flying like birds.'[37] In Israel Regardie's *The Golden Dawn* manuscripts, where much of this material is summarised, this advice is rendered a bit differently. 'Let him visualise it as something of a spherical shape, of a colour green, or blue, like the green leaves of a tree after rain, and carrying him with a mighty power away from the ground and flying in space like the birds. And let him repeat the syllable PAM.'[38]

I do not agree with some of these variations but include them here for the sake of completeness. According to the *Siva Samhita*, if you master the *Akasa Sanyama*, which it describes as 'contemplation on *sunya* (void, or vacuum, or space),' your body gradually will take on the qualities of the *Akasa*. It becomes 'altogether ethereal.' If you get to that point, you will be able to walk through walls, dive into the solid earth as if it were water, and so on. But do not be too expectant of these kinds of results. They are for the supreme masters of the art.[39]

I would also advise you, whatever results you achieve, not to demonstrate them to outsiders. Some people will be offended that you presume to do something that they cannot, while others will begin pestering you for psychic readings, advice on this and that, all of which becomes tiresome quickly. Siddhis are a private enjoyment. If you learn to float in the air, do it where nobody can see you. You will see the wisdom of that advice the first time you ignore it. I, for one, have a policy of giving absolutely no psychic demonstrations of any kind, although I occasionally use psychic principles to render aid incognito.

If you possibly can, set aside a regular time every day for practice and stick to it. If you cannot do that, you will find it useful to keep a diary showing the date and time of your practice sessions, how long you practised, and what exercises you performed. This will keep you from falling into the delusion that you have expended a great deal of effort with little result. If your effort is great, then your results will be great also. Your diary will help you to be honest with yourself.

And one final note: good luck!

CHAPTER NINE

SO YOU CAN FLY . . . NOW WHAT?

So you can fly . . . now what? Well, I'm not quite ready to let you go yet, because now that you understand the *Sanyama* technique, there are a lot of things you can do with it other than just fly. All of Book 3 of Patanjali's *Yoga Sutras* is devoted to more than two dozen siddhis that can be acquired through the practice of *Sanyama*. Some of them are minor, but others are almost as interesting as levitation. And those of you who are still trying to get into the full lotus may take comfort from the fact that some of these other siddhis are easier to do.

Now I cannot go into tedious detail concerning the rest of these siddhis, because there are so many of them. So what I am going to do is tell you what each of the sutras says, then explain briefly how each of the siddhis is performed. If you perform all the exercises I have given you thus far, by the time you are ready for the siddhis in this chapter, you should be able to fill in the blanks yourself.

The first of the siddhis is knowledge of the past and the future. In sutra number 16 of Book 3 Patanjali says that: 'By performing *sanyama* on the three kinds of changes comes knowledge of the past and the future.'

Almost everyone agrees that the 'three kinds of changes' refers to what philosophers call the three realities of time – past, present, and future, but there are several different interpretations of what meditation on these three kinds of changes will produce. Tibetan yogis perform this meditation in order to become intensely aware of the transitory nature of time. The present is but an infinitesimal interval separating two eternities – the past and the future. Scarcely has anyone a chance to appreciate the present moment before it has disappeared forever into the past. By sustained meditation on this fact, Tibetan occultists gradually come to realize that everything that exists in the present – which is everything – is just as transitory as the present in which they exist, including the world and the ego of man. It is easy enough to understand this fact at the intellectual level, but there is a more profound level of appreciation that emerges from long concentration, resulting in a radical alteration in one's view of the world – the state of mystical enlightenment.

A second interpretation is that by concentrating on the three realities, one gains intuitive knowledge of their intrinsic nature. I shall not expound on this further, because the knowledge that one acquires is so profound that it cannot be imparted intellectually. One must receive it in direct experience, through intuition. I will say, however, that those who enjoy meditation will really enjoy this one.

The third interpretation is that given by Alice Bailey in *The Light of the Soul*, that through this *Sanyama* 'comes the revelation of that which has been and of that which will be.' This is an area that I cannot go into too fully without exceeding the scope of this book. There is an intuitive apprehension of future events that can come through this meditation, but to perform it properly one needs a detailed knowledge of a certain branch of yogic occultism. As Rama Prasad said in *Nature's Finer Forces*:

Knowledge of the three times – the past, present and future – is nothing more than a scientific knowledge of the causes and effects of phenomena. Know the present *tattvic* state of things, know its antecedent and consequent states, and you have a knowledge of the three times.

In the seventeenth sutra, Patanjali says:

> Words, objects, and ideas appear to be the same thing because they occur together. Perform *Sanyama* on the difference between them and you will understand the cries of all living beings.

This is a very minor siddhi. As Patanjali points out, when we hear a word spoken, we tend to think of the sound of the word, the object that the word represents, and the mental idea in which both of those come together as being the same. Thus when we hear the sounds of beasts or the cries of birds we tend to feel that there is no *meaning* there. There is only the sound. Likewise, if we hear a person speaking in a language that we do not understand, we do not hear the meaning, only the sound. This can be overcome by listening to just the sound, without any mental effort to translate the sound into a meaning in an intellectual sense, and by *Sanyama* on the distinction between the sound, the meaning, and the idea, this can be done. One cannot then understand the language one has never studied, but one can understand the cries of beasts, because these cries represent basic drives and instincts. One can sense intuitively that this cry is a cry of anger, whereas that one is a cry of aggression. People who live around animals often acquire this siddhi incidentally, without ever consciously applying yoga.

The next sutra has to do with reincarnation. In sutra number eighteen, Patanjali says: 'Through awareness of subconscious tendencies, one attains knowledge of previous lifetimes.'

Anyone who has ever been exposed to very young babies or even baby animals knows that the personality at birth is already partially formed. Babies vary enormously in temperament, excitability, and intelligence, and one cannot escape the impression that these qualities must be inherited from previous births. By performing *Sanyama* on these qualities, the yogi finds clues to his previous lifetimes. This is especially possible with regard to strong tendencies and to certain kinds of phobias. For many years I was unable to use showers without strangling and had to come out of the shower every few seconds to breathe. By performing *Sanyama* on this tendency, I discovered that I had been gassed in my last lifetime in one of Hitler's concentration camps. This was simply an inherited characteristic that was related to a specific incident in a past life. If you can figure out which of your personality traits are inherited from previous lives, and strong interest in the occult usually is, by performing *Sanyama* on them, you may acquire knowledge of your previous births. I strongly recommend that you combine this siddhi with the mirror gazing exercise described in the last chapter. And one caution: the past-life insights that result from performance of this siddhi are flashes of intuition and not conclusions reached gradually. If you do *Sanyama* on some little quirk of yours and gradually come to the conclusion that you were this or that in your past life, or that you did something else, you are probably kidding yourself. Remember, *Sanyama* is not a process of analysis.

Our next siddhi has to do with mental telepathy. In the words of Patanjali: 'By *Sanyama* on the ideas, the yogi acquires knowledge of other men's minds.'

Now the trick here, as any telepath can tell you, is to make your mind receptive to impressions from other minds. And especially when you are just getting started, only attempt telepathy with someone you know and are friendly with. One very easy way to do this without anyone being the wiser is to ask a friend some question, then, before he has time to answer, try to become receptive to the thoughts going through his mind. If you are successful, you will have a definite impression of what he is going to tell you a split second before he has time to open his mouth. Then, when you get the answer, you have instant confirmation that your little experiment was successful. Later, you will learn to read people's minds at a distance. Once again, I have a little caution, though: you will find that you cannot use this power to invade another man's privacy. If you ask a question telepathically that the other fellow would not answer in person, you will not receive any impression, or, if you do, your impression will be unreliable. You will also find that you cannot contact a stranger telepathically who would rebuff you in person. And one last thing: do not ever challenge your subject to keep you from reading his mind. He is quite capable of doing so and your experiments will surely fail.

Now for an experiment in invisibility: 'By doing *Sanyama* on the form of the body, on the stopping of perceptibility, and on noncontact with the light of the eye, the yogi acquires the power of disappearance.'

This sutra describes one of the most difficult and magnificent of all the yogic powers. It is much more difficult to acquire than levitation, and it is at once more interesting. Invisibility is worthy of an entire book to itself, and for that reason shall occupy no more of our time here.

'By *Sanyama* on the two kinds of Karma, and on omens, comes knowledge of the time of death.'

It is said that to each man there is an allotted time to die, but that to no man is it given to know what that time is. The ancient Rosicrucians used to say of themselves that they were able to learn anything by means of art except the manner and time of their final departure. But it is possible, when the hour of death draws nigh, for the advanced yogi to sense it. Long before there is any outer sign, the astral body begins to separate itself from the physical, and the Inner Consciousness begins to adapt itself to the fact that life is coming to an end. People often become quite religious during these periods, and certain kinds of symbols begin to show up in their dreams: images of packing a suitcase, taking extended journeys, and so forth. Within a few days of death, the person may have some explicit dreams in which he is warned of his impending doom. When Socrates was arrested by the Areopagus, a youth of extraordinary beauty appeared to him in a dream and quoted a verse from Homer: 'Gladly on Pythia's shore the third day's dawn shall behold thee.' Thereafter he knew that he would be condemned and therefore disdained to conduct a spirited defence. Likewise with the yogis, they come by means of signs and portents to know that death is approaching, but never more than a year in advance.

In sutra number twenty-two Patanjali says: 'By performing *Sanyama* on Friendliness, there arises the power of Friendliness, etc.' This is one of the siddhis performed as a part of the TM-Sidhi Programme. According to Vyasas's commentary, this sutra applies to three sentiments: friendliness, compassion, and joy. The yogi feels friendliness for those who are happy, compassion for those who are in pain, and joy for those disposed to merit. By performing *Sanyama* on these three sentiments, the power of the sentiments is increased in the yogi, and the positive aspects of his personality are immeasurably enhanced.

Similar is sutra number twenty-three, where we read that: 'By *Sanyama* on the strength of an elephant, the yogi acquires it.'

This is the siddhi of Unlimited Strength. That this is possible becomes obvious from certain motor-car accidents, in which ordinary or even frail people have been seen to turn a motor-car aright without assistance, beat out petrol flames with their bare hands, and even bend twisted wreckage in an effort to rescue the victims. These powers manifest themselves in ordinary people only in times of dire emergency. The advanced yogi can summon them forth at will.

'By casting the light of higher sense-activity toward them, the yogi acquires knowledge of the subtle, the hidden, and the distant.'

Try it some time: when you have lost something, do not search for it at first, but sit down, close your eyes, and make your mind passive. Await some visual impression of where your lost treasures may be. Do not try to force an impression to come, for that will interfere with the necessary passivity of your mind. When your impression comes, go and search in the place indicated. If you have received a genuine psychic impression, you have manifested the siddhi in this sutra.

'By *Sanyama* on the Sun, the yogi acquires knowledge of the worlds.'

The worlds in this sutra refer to the *Lokas* in Hindu cosmology, which were not invented by early mythologists, as many orientalists believe, but apprehended directly through yogic powers. This is a very advanced siddhi and is not to be attempted by the beginner. The Adept is said to be able to project his awareness, not only to all parts of *this* world, but to all parts of all the other worlds as well. At pleasure he can observe what is going on there, and return to the world of men with full consciousness of his experiences. If anyone should foolishly try to acquire this siddhi, let me caution him not to look directly at the Sun in doing it. Perform *Sanyama* on a visualised mental image, lest you lose your ability to observe what is going on in this world.

A similar siddhi is described in the sutra following, to wit:

'By *Sanyama* on the Moon, the yogi learns about the system of the stars.'

The perception in this case remains within this universe but the principle is the same. In this case, one may do an open-eye *Sanyama* without danger, since the light of the Moon is not so brilliant as the light of the Sun. You will find that it works best during the Full Moon, since psychic abilities generally are strongest then. Some advanced students claim to have acquired a profound knowledge of the bases of astrology through this practice.

'By *Sanyama* on the Pole Star, the yogi learns about the movements of the stars.'

In Hindu cosmology, the Pole Star is said to be connected with all the other stars in the universe by means of 'wind-ropes' that are invisible, save to the gifted sight of the yogi. The stars revolve around the Pole Star, being carried about in a circle by these 'wind ropes.' In a paper called 'Plato, Piaget, and Maharishi on Cognitive Development,' published by the Maharishi International University in Fairfield, Iowa, Jonathan Shear reports on some very interesting research done by the TM organization into this sutra. It appears that not only do modern meditators all 'see' much the same thing when they meditate on the

Pole Star, but also what they 'see' is strikingly similar to what would be predicted by Hindu cosmology, and also to a certain vision related by Plato in *The Republic*. The universe appears as an umbrella-shaped device, with the Pole Star at the apex and the lesser stars suspended at various points along the umbrella-like surface, connected to the Pole Star with what one meditator described as 'bands of light.' I am not going to insist that these experiences have any objective validity, but it is interesting that a Greek in ancient Athens, Hindu yogis in ancient India, and TM meditators in Europe and the United States would all see the same thing and describe it the same way, without any communication having taken place between the three groups.

'By *Sanyama* on the Solar Plexus comes knowledge of the system of the body.'

There are various benefits to be derived from concentration on the Solar Plexus, but the specific benefit mentioned here is knowledge of the system of *nadis*. The *nadis* are psychic nerve channels, as it were, through which astral or *pranic* energy is carried throughout the body. There are seventy-two thousand important *nadis* in the body according to the yogic system, and all of them originate in the Solar Plexus. Thus the Solar Plexus becomes a storehouse of pranic energy. This energy radiates from the Solar Plexus to all parts of the body, just as, in the universe, pranic energy radiates from the Sun to all parts of the universe; thus the centre gets its name. By *Sanyama* on the Solar Plexus, the yogi intuitively knows, and eventually 'sees,' the system of *nadis* in the body.

'By *Sanyama* on the pit of the throat, the yogi passes beyond hunger and thirst.'

This siddhi simply results from the natural control over the body that the yogi acquires as a result of meditation on various parts of the body over a period of years, and also as a result of doing *asanas* and *pranayamas*. This Sanyama works extremely well and is quite easy for one properly prepared to do it. It does not, however, do away with the body's need for food and drink, only with the desire. Therefore, one must use common sense in applying this siddhi, lest the results be catastrophic.

'By Sanyama on the *Kurma-Nadi* (tortoise-tube), the yogi acquires stillness.'

The yogi is to imagine that below the well of the throat there is a tube that is shaped like a tortoise. By performing *Sanyama* on it, he is able to become aware of the subtle movements of the body to an extraordinary degree, and to acquire a bodily stillness that would not otherwise be possible. In·modern *Aikido* classes, something of the sort is achieved quite easily by maintaining the 'one-point' – sinking the consciousness into a point in the area of the Solar Plexus. The body then becomes perfectly still and immovable if the exercise is performed correctly. A person sitting in the full lotus, maintaining his awareness in the area of the Solar Plexus, cannot be tipped either forward or backward.

'By *Sanyama* on the light in the head, the yogi will see the *Siddhas*.'

The *Siddhas* are those who have passed before and who have acquired all the psychic abilities we are discussing, managing thereby to transcend all worldly cares and limitations. The *Siva Samhita* explains in more detail how this is done:

> When the yogi constantly imagines that he has a third eye – the eye of Siva – in the middle of his forehead, he then perceives a fire brilliant like lightning . . . If the experienced yogi thinks of this light day and night, he sees the *Siddhas*, and can certainly converse with them.

In the next sutra we read: 'Through the vividness of intuition the yogi knows all things.'

This simply refers to the power of 'refined intuition,' which can be developed through the cultivation of transcendental consciousness. By repeatedly consulting his intuition, the yogi strengthens it, until it becomes a real guide in his life. Through the use of it, he knows all things.

'By *Sanyama* on the heart, the yogi knows his own mind.'

The heart in this sutra naturally refers to the *Anahat Chakra*, which is located in the vicinity of the heart and that is thought, in Eastern countries, to be the physical location of the mind. Because the ancient Greeks decided that the mind was located in the brain, Western man thinks with his head, but Eastern man, following a different tradition, thinks with his heart. By watching closely the fluctuation in the 'mind-stuff' (*chitta*), the yogi acquires a knowledge of its workings. He understands how the principle of associations leads from one idea and mental concept to another. It was through an unconscious application of this particular *Sanyama* that the modern science of depth psychology came into being.

'Experience arises from failure to distinguish between objective reality (*sattva*) and the *purusha*, which is something quite different. *Sattva* exists as an object for something else. By *Sanyama* on the *purusha* comes knowledge of it.'

The commentaries explain that *sattva* refers to the mind, whereas *purusha* refers to the pure consciousness that lies behind the mind. One in effect performs this siddhi in meditation, when the thinking principle is transcended and the meditator enjoys the presence of pure awareness. This enjoyment can itself lead to siddhis, say the commentaries, principal among them being the development of five psychic senses.

'By loosening the causes of bondage, and by knowing the passages of the mind, the yogi may enter another's body.'

This siddhi is known technically as *Avesa*, and is mentioned frequently in early Theosophical literature, especially Colonel Olcott's book, *Old Diary Leaves*. The causes of bondage are the yogi's inherited karma. As his karmic debts become gradually paid, the yogi moves closer to the psychic condition in which he can perform *Avesa*. But this in itself is not enough. He must also know the passages of the mind, which in the commentaries are identified with the *nadis*, mentioned earlier. In practice, though, *Avesa* is quite easy for anyone who is skilled in astral projection and is often used either for purposes of psychic communication or else to implant noble impulses in the minds of persons who may be straying from their general high principles. The techniques whereby a person may be dominated psychically through *Avesa* are taught only to a selected few and would be worthless to undisciplined minds even if they were generally known.

Closely related to this siddhi is the siddhi described somewhat later in Patanjali's book, in sutra forty-two. We read: 'Actually passing out of the body and acting outside of it is the great discarnate. By this means the covering of light is removed.'

As I said in chapter 3 when I discussed astral projection, at first you will see as through a glass, darkly. This is because of the veil or covering of the interior light that the sutra speaks of. By practising projection again and again, the veil is gradually removed, and one sees clearly. However, we must not think in terms of that other veil, which hides the light of the self. That veil is removed by a higher siddhi developed through the practice of mysticism.

'By *Sanyama* on the *Samana*, the yogi becomes radiant.'

This means literally what it says. The *Samana* is one of the ten *Vayus* in the human body, and it is specifically one of the five that is involved in occult powers. It is situated in the area of the stomach and is involved in the digestion of food. It is the home of the Fire Element (*Tejas Tattwa*) in the human body, and can produce several remarkable effects. The effulgence spoken of here is merely an intensification of the human aura, so that it becomes visible to the profane.

'By *Sanyama* on the relationship between the *Akasa* and the sense of hearing becomes supernormal hearing.'

The five *Tattwas* in Hindu theory are the basis of the five *Indriyas*, or senses. Thus the Fire Element, the *Tejas Tattwa*, is the basis for the sense of sight, and the *Akasa Tattwa* is the basis for the sense of hearing. The commentaries say that by *Sanyama* on the other elements, other supernormal senses can be acquired as well. Thus, by *Sanyama* on Water, super-tasting; by *Sanyama* on the Earth Element, super-smell; and so on. The most common result of this siddhi is not clairaudience but the hearing of the *Anahat* – the Voice of the *Nadis* – mystical sounds that become audible to the yogi in deep concentration. Ten of these sounds are classically named, ranging from the hum of the honey bee to the sound of thunder. It is customary when doing this *Sanyama* to put your fingers in your ears and listen for the sounds. When they come – and it may take some time before you start to hear them – use them as a focus of concentration. That is, direct your attention toward the sounds, and do not allow it to wander. When it does wander, as it will at first, gently bring your attention back to the sounds. In time the sounds will become more intense, which indicates that the practice is succeeding. Thus do some yogis gain one-pointedness.

If you want to experiment with some of these siddhis, let me suggest that you select just one and work with just that one siddhi once a day every day for at least six months. Do not hesitate to experiment with the techniques, because experimentation is an essential part of the learning process, particularly if you are learning from a book. Within six months, if you are performing the experiments correctly, you should begin to have some spontaneous experiences. The siddhis will not be under control yet – that is the mark of the master, and can take some time. But you should begin to have some occasional siddhi experiences. And in your moments of dire need you will discover that you have acquired a power that will come to your aid in some rather strange ways. These are all signs of progress. In time you will acquire the mastery you desire.

Now I am going to tell you something that will be meaningless to the beginners among you, but that the Adepts will understand only too well. There will come a time, after you have acquired a certain degree of mastery over the siddhis, when you will want to renounce them. This is not because they will be any burden to you but because of a certain parallel level of development that will occur in you because of the exercises you will be performing. It is characteristic of human nature that whenever one climbs a mountain, it ceases to be of interest. One wants to climb another mountain that is higher and more difficult. I say this not because you will understand it now, but because I want to plant a seed as it were in your mind. When you have climbed the first mountain in yoga – the siddhis – you will find that the bottom of the next higher mountain becomes visible. And if, as I hope, you attempt to climb that mountain, you will reap the very highest benefits yoga has to offer. And in doing so, you will find out what this ancient science is really all about.

APPENDIX

Forty Levitated Persons, Canonised or Beatified

From The Quarterly Journal of Science *(February, 1875),*
Compiled by Sir William Crookes

Name, Country, and Condition	Dates	Citations in 'The Acta-Sanctorium'		
	Dates	Month	Volume	Page
Andrew Salus, Scythian Slave	880–946	May	VI	16
Luke of Soterium, Greek Monk	890–946	Feb	II	85
Stephen I, King of Hungary	978–1038	Sept	I	541
Ladislas I, King of Hungary	1041–1096	June	V	318
Christina, Flemish Nun	1150–1220	July	V	656
St. Dominic, Italian Preacher	1170–1221	Aug	I	405, 573
Lurgard, Belgian Nun	1182–1246	June	III	238
Agnes of Bohemia, Princess	1205–1281	March	I	522
Humiliana of Florence, Widow	1219–1246	May	IV	396

Jutta, Prussian Widow, Hermit	1215–1264	May	VII	606
St. Bonaventura, Italian Cardinal	1221–1274	July	III	827
St. Thomas Aquinas, Italian Friar	1227–1274	March	I	670–81
Ambrose Sausedonius, Italian Priest	1220–1287	March	III	192
Peter Armengol, Spanish Priest	1238–1304	Sept	I	334
St. Albert, Sicilian Priest	1240–1306	Aug	II	236
Princess Margaret of Hungary	1242–1270	Jan	II	904
Robert of Solentium, Italian Abbot	1273–1341	July	IV	503
Agnes of Mt, Politian, Italian Abbess	1274–1317	April	II	794
Bartholus of Vado, Italian Hermit	?–1300	June	II	1007
Princess Elizabeth of Hungary	1297–1338	May	II	126
Catharine Columbina, Spanish Abbess	?–1387	July	VII	352
St. Vincent Ferrer, Spanish Missionary	1359–1419	April	I	497
Coleta of Ghent, Flemish Abbess	1381–1447	March	I	559, 576
Jeremy of Panormo, Sicilian Friar	1381–1452	March	I	297
St. Antonine, Archbishop of Florence	1389–1459	May	I	335
St. Francis of Paola, Missionary	1440–1507	April	I	117
Osanna of Mantus, Italian Nun	1450–1505	June	III	703, 705

Bartholomew of Anghiers, Friar	?–1510	March	II	665
Columba of Ricci, Italian Nun	1468–1501	May	V	332–34, 360
Thomas, Archbishop of Valencia	1487–1555	Sept	V	832–969
St. Ignatius Loyola, Spanish Soldier	1491–1556	July	VII	432
Peter of Alcantara, Spanish Friar	1499–1562	Oct	VIII	672–73, 687
St. Philip Neri, Italian Friar	1515–1597	May	VI	590
Salvator de Horta, Spanish Friar	1520–1567	March	II	679–80
St. Luis Bertrand, Spanish Missionary	1526–1581	Oct	V	407, 483
St. Theresa, Spanish Abbess	1515–1582	Oct	VII	399
John a' Cruce, Spanish Priest	1542–1591	Oct	VII	239
J. S. Piscator, Roman Professor	?–1586	June	IV	976
Joseph of Cupertino, Italian Friar	1603–1663	Sept	V	1020–22
Bonaventura of Potenza, Italian Friar	1651–1711	Oct	XII	154

NOTES

Chapter 1

1. Frank Kaleda, *The Shining Ones*. Privately published. Kent, Ohio, 1978. Pages not numbered.

2. Dr. Herbert Benson, *The Relaxation Response*. New York: William Morrow & Co., 1975, pp. 120–121.

3. Rick Fields, 'Levitation for the Masses,' *New Age*, July 1977, p. 52.

4. Jody Gaylin, 'I'm the Maharishi – Fly Me,' *Psychology Today*, August 1977, pp. 29, 85.

5. Robert W. Neuben, 'Magician Doug Henning: "There Is Real Magic . . . ,"' *New Realities*, August 1978, p. 13.

6. David Fetcho, 'New Flights of Fancy,' *Spiritual Counterfeits Project Newsletter*, June 1977. Pages not numbered.

7. Michael Hellicar, 'Maharishi's Flying Circus,' *The Daily Mirror*, 14 July 1977, p. 5.

8. Douglas Sagi, 'TM. "More Than a Hop Away,"' *The Vancouver Sun*, 15 December 1977.

9. Michael Hellicar, op. cit.

10. Kenneth L. Woodward and Pamela Abramson, 'Maharishi Over Matter,' *Newsweek*, 13 June 1977.

11. Eugene L. Meyer, 'New High from the Maharishi: Levitation from Meditation,' *The Washington Post*, 6 June 1977.

12. John Dart, 'TM Ruled Religious, Banned in Schools,' *The Los Angeles Times*, 29 October 1977.

13. Ibid.

14. 'Seer of Flying,' *Time Magazine*, 8 August 1977, p. 75.

15. Aubrey B. Haines, 'Taking A Flier With TM,' *The Christian Century*, 16–23 August 1978, pp. 770–71.

16. Swami Vishnu Devananda, *Meditation and Mantras*. New York: OM Lotus Publishing Company, 1978, p. 185.

17. Cherly Smith, 'Swami Denounces TM for its "Pay Now, Fly Later" Promotion', *The News World* (New York), 11 August 1977.

18. Rick Fidds, op. cit.

Chapter 2

1. Quoted by H. P. Blavatsky in *Isis Unveiled*, vol. 1, p. xxiv. Los Angeles: The Theosophy Company, 1968.

2. Sir Arthur Eddington, *Space, Time, and Gravitation*. Cambridge University Press, 1966.

3. H. G. Wells, 'The First Men in the Moon,' in *The Works of H. G. Wells*, vol. 6. New York: Charles Scribner, 1905.

4. George Gamow, *Gravity*. New York: Doubleday, 1962.

5. D. C. Peaslee, 'Non-existence of Gravity Shields,' *Science*, 28 December 1956.

6. John Bigelow, *Frogstein's Saucer Technology*. Mokelumne Hill, California: Health Research, 1975.

7. Robert L. Forward, 'A New Gravity Field,' *Science Digest*, September, 1962, pp. 73–78.

8. Betty Jo Dobbs, *The Foundations of Newton's Alchemy*. London: Cambridge University Press, 1975, p. 210.

9. Cyrus Teed, *The Cellular Cosmogony*, Estero, Florida: The Guiding Star Publishing House, 1905, reprinted by The Porcupine Press, Philadelphia, 1975. Quote taken from preface, no page numbers.

10. Ibid., p. 164.

11. 'Oh, Mr. Copernicus!,' *Time*, 14 July 1947.

Chapter 3

1. H. P. Blavatsky, *Isis Unveiled*, vol. 1, p. 495.

2. Montague Summers, *A Popular History of Witchcraft*. New York: Causeway Books, 1973.

3. David Brewster, *Letters on Natural Magic*, London: J. Murray, 1832.

4. 'The Famous History of Friar Bacon,' in *Some Old English Worthies*, edited by Dorothy Senior. London: Stephen Swift & Co., 1952, p. 202.

5. Ibid., pp. 22–23.

6. W. Y. Evans-Wentz, *Tibet's Great Yogi Milarepa*. London: Oxford University Press, 1969, p. 212.

7. Alexandra David-Neel, *Magic and Mystery in Tibet*. New Hyde Park, New York: University Books, 1965, pp. 194–95.

8. Eunapius, *Lives of the Philosophers*, translated by W. C. Wright. London: W. Heinemann, 1922.

9. Iamblichus, *On the Mysteries*, quoted by H. P. Blavatsky in *Isis Unveiled*, vol. 1, p. 219.

10. Patanjali, *Yoga Sutras*, 3.37. The numbering of the Sutras varies from one translation to the next.

11. Ansari of Herat, *The Invocations of Shekh Abdullah Ansari of Herat*, translated by Sardar Sir Jogendra Singh. London, 1939. Quoted by Aldous Huxley in *The Perennial Philosophy*. London: Harper & Bros. 1945, p. 259.

12. Ibid.

13. Quoted by Andrew Lang, *Cock Lane and Common-Sense*. London: Longman Green & Co., 1901, p. 105.

14. Olivier Leroy, *Levitation, An Examination of the Evidence and Explanations*. London: B. Oates & Washbourne, 1928.

15. Sir William Crookes, *The Quarterly Journal of Science*, January 1875.

16. Ernest Wood, *Yoga*. New York: Penguin Books, 1960.

17. Philostratus, *The Life of Apollonius of Tyana*, translated by F. C. Conybeare. London: W. Heinemann, 1912.

18. Quoted by Colonel Yule in *The Book of Ser. Marco Polo*. New York: Charles Scribner, 1926, p. 315.

19. Quoted by Yule, p. 316.

20. Professor Harry Kellar, 'High Caste Indian Magic,' *The North American Review*, 1893, vol. clvi, pp. 75 et seq.

21. Quoted by Yule, pp. 316–17.

22. Blavatsky, *Isis Unveiled*, vol. l, p. 115.

23. James Webb, *The Occult Underground*. La Salle, Illinois: The Open Court Publishing Company, 1974, p. 135.

24. Indrija Puharich, *Beyond Telepathy*. Garden City, New York: Doubleday, 1962.

25. Quoted in *Extrasensory Ecology; Parapsychology and Anthropology*, edited by Joseph K. Long. London: The Scarecrow Press, 1977.

26. Louis Jacolliot, *Occult Science in India and Among the Ancients*, translated by W. L. Felt. London: Rider, 1919.

27. 'The Sishals and Bhukailas Yogis,' translated by Babu Rajnarain Bose, *The Theosophist*, August 1882, p. 274.

28. *The Illustrated London News*, 6 June 1936, pp. 993–95.

29. Seenath Chatterjee, 'A Self-Levitated Lama,' *The Theosophist*. September 1887, pp. 726–28.

30. D. H. Rawcliffe, *Occult and Supernatural Phenomenon*. New York: Dover, 1959, p. 281.

31. Mircea Eliade, *Yoga, Immortality, and Freedom*. Princeton, New Jersey: Princeton University Press, 1969, p. 277.

32. Summers, *A Popular History of Witchcraft*, p. 138.

33. *The Book of the Sacred Magic of Abra-Melin the Mage*, translated by S. L. MacGregor Mathers. New York: Dover, 1975, pp. 20–21.

34. Quoted by Reginald Scot in Scot's *Discoverie of Witchcraft*. London, 1651, book x, chapter viii.

35. Lynn Schroeder and Sheila Ostrander, *Psychic Discoveries Behind the Iron Curtain*. New York: Bantam Books, 1970, p. 250.

36. Arthur Avalon (Sir John Woodroffe), *The Serpent Power*, New York: Dover, 1974, p. 382.

37. Quoted by Richard Scott in *Transcendental Misconceptions*. San Diego, California: Beta Books, 1978, p. 111.

38. Arthur Edward Waite, *The Real History of the Rosicrucians*. London: George Redway, 1887, p. 409.

39. Havelock Ellis, 'Aviation in Dreams,' *Atlantic Monthly*, October, 1910, pp. 474–75.

40. H. Spencer Lewis, *Rosicrucian Questions and Answers*, San Jose, California: Supreme Grand Lodge AMORC, 1971, p. 59.

41. Havelock Ellis, p. 469.

42. Andrew Lang, pp. 99–100.

Chapter 4

1. *Siva Samhita*, translated by Srisachandra Vasu. Allahabad, India: The Indian Press, 1914, pp. 64, 67–68, 84–85, 190–91, 203; on the chakras see also *The Gheranda Samhita*, also translated by Srisachandra Vasu. Allahabad, India: The Indian Press, 1914.

2. Mouni Sadhu, *The Tarot*. Hollywood, California: Wilshire Book Co., 1971, pp. 65–66.

3. Harold Bloomfield, *Happiness: The TM Programme, Psychiatry, and Enlightenment*. New York: Dawn Press, 1976, p. 52.

4. E.A.T.W. Budge, *Egyptian Magic*. London: K. Paul, Trench, and Trubner, 1899.

5. Origen, *Contra Celsum*, translated by Henry Chadwick. Cambridge University Press, 1953, 1.24.

6. Plutarch, *Isis and Osiris*, translated by F. C. Babbitt, in *Plutarch's Monalia*, vol. 5, p. 25. London: W. Heinemann, 1927.

7. Swami Vivekananda, *The Complete Works of Swami Vivekananda*. Calcutta: Advaita Ashram, 1971–73, vol. 3, p. 58.

8. Quoted in William James, *The Varieties of Religious Experience*. New York: New American Library, 1958, p. 295n.

9. Norman Vincent Peale, *The Power of Positive Thinking*. New York: Prentice Hall, 1952, pp. 23–24.

10. Maharishi Mahesh Yogi, *Meditations*. New York: Bantam Books, 1968.

11. Harold Bloomfield et al., *TM: Discovering Inner Energy and Overcoming Stress*. New York: Dell Publishing Company, 1975, p. 45.

12. Bloomfield, *Happiness*, p. 81.

13. Adam Smith, 'The Meditation Game,' *Atlantic*, October 1975, pp. 33–45; William Whalen, reprinted in *Science Digest*. August 1977. p. 37, from *U.S. Catholic*; John Weldon and Zola Levitt, *The Transcendental Explosion*. Irvine, California: Harvest House Publishers, 1976, pp. 190, 193; Frank Kaleda, 'The Shining Ones,' *Time* magazine, 3 November 1975, p. 6; R. D. Scott, *Transcendental Misconceptions*. San Diego. California: Beta Books, 1978, pp. 45–54, 89–99; 'Who Is This Man and What Does He Want?,' circular published by The Spiritual Counterfeits Project, Berkeley, California; Nicholas Regush, 'You Can't Learn to Walk Through Walls,' *Sunday Express* (Montreal), 21 May 1978; This is only a partial list of publications in which TM mantras have been disclosed.

14. Loudon Wainwright, 'Invitation to Instant Bliss,' *Life*, 10 November 1967, p. 26.

15. Maharishi Mahesh Yogi, *Meditations*.

16. Frank Kaleda, *The Shining Ones*.

17. Alain Danielou, *Hindu Polytheism*, quoted by R. D. Scott in *Transcendental Misconceptions*, pp. 92–93.

18. 'TM: Penetrating the Veil of Deception,' anti-TM pamphlet published by The Spiritual Counterfeits Project, published sans date or page numbers.

19. Ibid.

20. Benson, *The Relaxation Response*, pp. 113–14.

21. Lydiard Horton, 'The Illusion of Levitation,' *Journal of Abnormal Psychology*, vol. 13, p. 50.

22. *The Secret of the Golden Flower*, translated by Richard Wilhelm. New York: Causeway Books, 1931, p. 56.

23. Freda Morris, PhD., 'Self-Hypnosis for Meditation,' in *TM: How to Find Peace of Mind Through Meditation*, edited by Martin Ebon. New York: New American Library, 1976, p. 225.

Chapter 5

1. *The Acts of Peter*, translated by Montague Rhodes James, published in *The Apocryphal New Testament*. Oxford University Press, reprinted 1966, p. 307.

2. H. P. Blavatsky, *Isis Unveiled*, vol. l, p. xxiii.

3. Swami Vivekananda, *Complete Works*, vol. l, p. 508.

4. Professor Harry Kellar, op. cit., p. 81.

5. Ibid.

6. H. P. Blavatsky, *Isis Unveiled*, vol. l, pp. xxiii–iv.

7. H. P. Blavatsky in *The Theosophist*, August 1882, p. 272.

8. H. P. Blavatsky, *Isis Unveiled*, vol. l, pp. 497–98.

9. T. H. Huxley, 'Scientific and Pseudo-Scientific Realism,' *The Nineteenth Century*, February 1887, p. 202.

10. Swami Vivekananda, vol. 1, pp. 503, 506.

11. Swami Vishnu Devananda, *The Complete Illustrated Book of Yoga*. New York: Pocket Books, 1972, p. 240.

Chapter 6

1. *Dighanikaya*, I, 78 et seq., quoted by Mircea Eliade in *Patanjali and Yoga*, translated by C. L. Markmann. New York: Schocken Books, 1975, p. 173.

2. Quoted by Yule, *Marco Polo*, p. 315.

3. *Siva Samhita*, 3.42, p. 31.

4. Edmund Jacobson, *You Must Relax*. New York & London: Whittlesey House, McGraw Hill, 1934.

5. *Hatha Yoga Pradipika*, translated by Pancham Sinh. Allahabad: Indian Press, 1915, p. 15.

6. *Siva Samhita*, 3.40–41, p. 30.

7. *Gheranda Samhita*, 5.56, p. 45.

8. Ibid., 5.55, p. 45.

9. Arthur Avalon, *The Serpent Power*, p. 216.

10. Theos Bernard, *Hatha Yoga: The Report of a Personal Experience*. New York: Weiser, 1975, p. 58.

11. *Siva Samhita*, 5.64, p. 64.

12. *Siva Samhita*, 3.46, p. 31.

13. Aleister Crowley, *The Confessions of Aleister Crowley*. New York: Bantam Books, 1971, p. 247.

14. Hereward Carrington, *Higher Psychic Development*. Aquarian Press, 1978.

15. Crowley, op. cit., p. 247.

16. Paramahansa Yogananda, *The Autobiography of a Yogi*. Los Angeles: Self Realization Fellowship, 1969, p. 63.

17. I. K. Taimini, *The Science of Yoga*. Adyar, Madras, India: The Theosophical Publishing House, 1974, pp. 311, 346.

18. Idries Shah, *Oriental Magic*. London: Rider, 1956, p. 140.

19. Thelma Moss, *The Probability of the Impossible*. Los Angeles: J. P. Tarcher, Inc., 1974, pp. 133–35.

20. Fosco Maraini, *Secret Tibet*. London: Hutchinson & Co., Ltd., 1952, p. 53

21. Seenath Chatterjee, 'A Self-Levitated Lama,' *The Theosophist*, September 1887, pp. 726–28.

22. Joshi Ootamram Doolabrahm, 'Another Aethrobar,' *The Theosophist*, April, 1880, p. 184.

Chapter 7

1. H. P. Blavatsky, *Isis Unveiled*, vol. 1, p. 500.

2. W. Y. Evans-Wentz, *Tibetan Yoga Secret Doctrines*. Oxford University Press, 1958, p. xxxiii.

3. *Hatha Yoga Pradipika*, chapter V, sutra 24, p. 50.

4. W. Y. Evans-Wentz, *Tibetan Yoga*, p. xxviii.

5. Aristotle, *On the Soul*, book 1, chap. 5, 30, translated by J. A Smith in *The Basic Works of Aristotle*. New York: Random House, 1941, p. 552.

6. Conway Zirkle, 'Animals Impregnated by the Wind,' *Isis*, vol. 26 (1937), pp. 95 et seq.

7. C. G. Jung, 'Basic Postulates of Analytical Psychology,' in *The Collected Works of C. G. Jung*. New York: Pantheon Books, 1960, vol. 8, p. 345.

8. Ibid.

9. Evans-Wentz, *Tibetan Yoga*, pp. xxix-xxx.

10. Alexander Cannon, *The Invisible Influence*. London: Rider, 1934.

11. Ernest Wood, *Practical Yoga, Ancient and Modern*. New York: E. P. Dutton & Co., 1948, p. 120n.

12. Bloomfield, *Happiness*, p. 57; Robert Keith Wallace, 'Physiological Effects of Transcendental Meditation,' *Science*, 27 March 1970, vol. 167, pp. 1751–54.

13. H. Spencer Lewis, 'The Mystical Meaning of AMEN,' *The Rosicrucian Digest*. February 1976, p. 25.

14. Rama Prasad, *Nature's Finer Forces*. Adyar, Madras, India: The Theosophical Publishing House, p. 216.

15. Schroeder and Ostrander, *Psychic Discoveries*, p. 291.

16. Joseph Weed, *The Wisdom of the Mystic Masters*. West Nyack, New York: Parker Publishing Company, 1968, p. 161.

17. Michael Minick, *The Wisdom of Kung-Fu*. New York: Warner Books, 1975, pp. 60–61.

18. Michael Murphy and Rhen A. White, *The Psychic Side of Sports*. Reading, Massachusetts: Addison-Wesley, 1970, p. 101.

19. Schroeder and Ostrander, *Psychic Discoveries*, p. 250.

20. Karel Weiner, *Yoga and Indian Philosophy*. Delhi, India: Motilal Banarsidass, 1977, pp. 68–69.

21. Maharishi Mahesh Yogi, *On the Bhagavad-Gita*. Middlesex: Penguin Books, 1976, pp. 144, 147, 150, 465, etc.

22. Rama Prasad, *Nature's Finer Forces*, p. 239.

Chapter 8

1. W. Y. Evans-Wentz, *Tibetan Yoga*, p. 118.

2. *Siva Samhita*, 3.57, p. 33.

3. Swami Vivekananda, vol. 8, p. 194.

4. Maharishi Mahesh Yogi, *Transcendental Meditation* (formerly titled *The Science of Being and Art of Living*). New York: New American Library, 1968, pp. 47–48.

5. Maharishi Mahesh Yogi, *TM*, pp. 98–99.

6. A. J. Deikman, 'Implications of Experimentally Induced Contemplative Levitation,' *Journal of Nervous and Mental Disease*, vol. 142, 1966, p. 101.

7. A. J. Deikman, p. 105.

8. Aleister Crowley, *The Confessions of Aleister Crowley*, p. 243.

9. John Weldon and Zola Levitt, *The Transcendental Explosion*. Irvine, California: Harvest House Publishers, 1976, p. 199.

10. Colin Bennett, *Practical Time Travel*. London: The Aquarian Press Ltd., 1971, p. 28.

11. Ibid.

12. Max Freedom Long. *Recovering the Ancient Magic*. London: Rider, 1936.

13. Mircea Eliade, *Yoga*, p. 77.

14. David W. Orme-Johnson et al., 'The Effects of the Age of Enlightenment Governor Training Courses on Field Independence, Creativity, Intelligence . . .' p. 715, paper 103, Scientific Research on the TM Programme, MERU Press.

15. Evans-Wentz, *Tibetan Yoga*, p. 77.

16. *Gheranda Samhita*, 5.65, p. 47.

17. Alice Bailey, *The Light of the Soul*. New York: Lucis Publishing Company, 1955, p. 330.

18. I. K. Taimni, p. 346.

19. Alice Bailey, p. 330.

20. *The Yoga Sutras of Patanjali*, vol. lv of *The Sacred Books of the Hindus*. Allahabad: Indian Press, 1912, p. 239.

21. Ibid.

22. *An Invitation to Enlightenment*. Maharishi International University, 1977, p. 94.

23. David W. Orme-Johnson et al., 'Higher States of Consciousness: EEG Coherence, Creativity, and Experiences of the Sidhis,' p. 705, paper 102, *Scientific Research on the TM Programme*.

24. Maharishi Mahesh Yogi, *On the Bhagavad-Gita*, p. 486.

25. David Orme-Johnson, 'The Dawn of the Age of Enlightenment: Experimental Evidence that the Transcendental Meditation Technique Produces a Fourth and Fifth State of Consciousness . . .,' pp. 671 et seq., paper 100, *Scientific Research on the TM Programme*.

26. Edward Conze, *Buddhist Scriptum*. Baltimore: Penguin Books, 1959, p. 128.

27. *Siva Samhita*, 1.51. p. 8.

28. Robert W. Neubert, 'Magician Doug Henning . . . ,' p. 13.

29. Orme-Johnson, 'Higher States of Consciousness . . . ,' p. 708.

30. Joseph Weed, *The Wisdom of the Mystic Masters*, p. 162.

31. Hugo Muensterberg, *Psychotherapy*. New York: Moffat, Yard, & Co., 1909, pp. 315–17.

32. Orme-Johnson, 'Higher States of Consciousness . . . ,' p. 708.

33. Rama Prasad, *Nature's Finer Forces*, p. 237.

34. Ibid.

35. T. R. Srinivasa Ayyangar, *Yoga Upanishads*. Adyar, Madras, India: The Theosophical Publishing House, 1952.

36. *Gheranda Samhita*, pp. 32–33.

37. Rama Prasad, *Nature's Finer Forces*, p. 237.

38. Israel Regardie, *The Golden Dawn*. St. Paul, Minnesota: Llewellyn Publications, 1971, vol. 4, p. 105.

39. *Siva Samhita*, 5.47, p. 61.

INDEX

Abraham the Jew, 34
Acta Sanctorum, 27
Adhama, 77
Ajna Chakra, 24, 47
Akasa, 65, 113, 115, 116, 119,
    120–23
Akhnaton, 42
AMORC, 37, 42
Anahat Chakra, 36, 37, 45, 134
Ansari of Herat, 25
Apana, 110
Apollonius of Tyana, 28
Asanas, 9, 56, 71, 132
Astral body, 41, 86, 90, 94, 129
Astral projection, 1, 37–42, 46, 112,
    134
Avalon, Arthur, 77, 113, 121

Bailey, Alice, 111, 126
Bennett, Colin, 106
Benson, Dr. Herbert, 3, 54
Berkeley Christian Coalition, 51
Bernard, Dr. Theos, 78
Bey, Tahra, 95
Bhaduri, Nagendra Nath, 80
Bharati, Aghenandra, 32
Bhuchari-Siddhi, see
    Dardhuri-Siddhi
Bigelow, John, 14
Birdsell, David, 106
Blavatsky, H. P., 17, 23, 31, 61–62,
    85
Bloomfield, Dr. Harold, 45
*Book of the Sacred Magic of Abra-
    melin the Mage*, 34–35

Brahma, 47
Brewster, Sir David, 24
Buddha, 26, 69

Cakasagamanam, 115, 119
Cannon, Alexander, 87
Carrington, Hereward, 79
'Cellular cosmogony,' 16
Chakras, 46, 78, 120
Chatterjee, Seenath, 82
Cloud of Unknowing, The, 48
Committee for the Sincere Practice
    of Yoga, 7
Coomaraswamy, 33
Copernicus, 17
Cosmic Consciousness (CC), 52,
    115
Crowley, Aleister, 79, 106
Cupertino, Joseph of, 1

Damis, 28
Darduri-Siddhi ('frog-jump power'),
    78
David-Neel, Alexandra, 25
de Chazal, Comte, 41
Deikman, Dr. A. J., 106
de Pasqually, Martinez, 36
Devadatta, 110
Devananda, Swami Vishnu, 7–8, 66
Dhananjaya, 110
Dharana, 103–9
Dhyana, 107–9, 114
Diaphragmatic breathing (D-
    breathing), 72
Dighanikaya, The, 26, 69

Domash, Lawrence, 51
Doolabrahm, Joshi Ootamram, 83
Drogzenovich, Mikhail, 91

Eckankar, 37
Eclectic Medical College, 16
Eddington, Arthur, 12
Einstein, Albert, 16, 18, 20–22
Ellis, Havelock, 42
Enlightenment, state of, 2, 4–5, 87, 114, 126
Eunapius, 25
Evans-Wentz, W. Y., 85, 109

Fields, Rick, 10
Flying ointments, 34–36
Fodor, Nandor, 92
Forward, Robert, 14
Frogstein Papers, 14
Frogstein's Saucer Technology, 13
Full lotus, see *Padmasana*

Gamow, Dr. George, 13
Gheranda Samhita, 77, 110, 122–123
'Governor Training Course of the Age of Enlightenment,' 5
Gravity, 11–15, 17–20, 22, 61–63, 66, 81
Grilland, Paul, 34
Guru Dev, 54

Haines, Aubrey, 8
Hellicar, Michael, 7
Henning, Doug, 5
Home, Daniel Dunglas, 43
Horton, Lydiard, 55
Houdin, Robert, 34
Huxley, Aldous, 26
Huxley, Thomas Henry, 63–64

Iamblichus, 25–26
Ida, 89
Imbert-Gourbeyre, Dr., 24
Indian Rope Trick, 30, 32
Invisibility, 2, 4, 129

Jacobson, Edmond, 73
James, William, 23
Japa, 33, 100, 114, 122
Jiva, 94,

Kaleda, Frank, 51, 53
Karana sharita, 94
Kayakasayoh, 115, 119
Kellar, Professor, 29, 61
'Koreshan Unity,' 16
Krikara, 110
Kshanika-samadhi, 114–15
Kumbhaka, 75, 77
Kundalini, 9, 71, 78
Kurma, 110, 133

Laghima, 119
Lang, Andrew, 42
Lauro, Ling Lau, 34
Leroy, Olivier, 27
Levitt, Zola, 51, 106
Linga sharira, 94
Long, Max Freedom, 107, 109, 122

Macey, John, 10
Madhyama, 77
Magus, Simon, 59–60
Maharishi European Research University, 3–8
Maharishi International University, 8
Maharishi Mahesh Yogi, 1, 2–4, 6, 8, 49–51, 54, 93, 102–3, 113–15, 118
Mahendra, Prince, 28
Manas, 94
Mantras, 45–46, 49–53, 55, 89, 102
Mantra Shastras, 53
Maraini, Fosco, 81–82
Masyasana, 71
Melton, Edward, 30, 32
Menninger Clinic, 40
Milarepa, 24–25
Minick, Michael, 92
Moon Breath, 88–90
Morrow, U. G., 17
Moss, Thelma, 81

Muensterberg, Hugo, 117–18
Muladhara Chakra, 45, 78
Murphy, Michael, 92

Nadis, 76, 132, 134, 136
Naga, 110
Nagarjuna, 34
Navarro, Antonio Duran, 17–18
Neopolitanus, Johannes Baptista, 35
Newton, Sir Isaac, 12, 15–16, 18–20,
    65
    Second Law of Motion, 18
Nijinsky, 92
Nitya; 115
Nitya-samadhi, 115

Olcott, Colonel, 24, 134
Origen, 46
Orme-Johnson, David, 108, 114,
    118
Ostrander, Sheila, 36, 91

Padmasana, 69–71, 74, 78, 82
'Party levitation,' 80–81
Patanjali, 4, 25, 100, 106–7, 111,
    113–14, 116, 125–28, 130, 135
Peale, Dr. Norman, 49
Peaslee, D. C., 13
Pepper, Bob, 6
Philostratus, 28
Pingala, 89
Plunkett, P. T., 33
Plutarch, 46
Porphyry, 26
Prabandhacintamani, 34
Prana, 5, 9, 64–67, 85–87, 91, 93,
    95–97, 99, 111, 121
Pranayama, 5, 61–62, 64, 74–81, 85,
    94, 99–101, 118–19, 132
Prasad, Rama, 90, 95, 122–23, 126
Pratyahara, 100–103
Puharich, Dr. Indrija, 32
Pullavar, Subbayah, 33
Puraka, 75, 77, 95
Puraka-Kumbhaka-Rechaka (PKR)
    ratios, 76–77

Rechaka, 75
Regardie, Israel, 123
Regush, Nicholas, 52
Rozman, Stephen, vii, 5–6
Russell, Bertrand, 26

Sadhu, Mouni, 45
Sahasrara Chakra, 110, 120
Samadhi, 87, 107–9, 114–115, 117, 121
Samana, 110, 121, 135
Sanyama, 99, 107–11, 113–14,
    116–18, 121–23, 125–36
Schroeder, Lynn, 36, 91
Scott, R. D., 52
Scott, Susan, 52
Secret of the Golden Flower, The, 55
Seelisberg, 3–4
Sepher Yezirah, 47
Serpent Power, The, 37, 45, 77
Shah, Idries, 81
Shiva, 47
Siddhis, 1–5, 9, 25–26, 82, 96, 99,
    103, 109, 114–15, 123, 125, 130,
    134, 136–37
Silva Mind Control, 37
Sishal, 33–34
Sivagama, The, 95, 123
Siva Samhita, 45, 65, 76, 78, 100,
    113, 117, 119, 133
Smith, Adam, 50
Spencer, Lewis, Dr. H., 42, 89
Spiritual Counterfeits Project, 51, 53
Sun Breath, 88–90
Sykes, David, 7

Taimni, I. K., 80, 111
Tattwas, 119–22, 135
Teed, Cyrus, 16–17
Tennyson, Alfred, Lord, 48, 56
TM-Sidhi Programme, 2, 5, 79, 109,
    114, 130
Transcendental consciousness (TC),
    93, 114–15, 133

Udana, 110–13, 118, 121
Urban, Dr. Rudolph von, 32
Uttama, 77

Vachaspati, 110–11

Valentyn, Francis, 28

Vayus, 110, 113, 121, 135

Verrill, David, 7

Victoria, Queen, 29

Vishnu, 7–8, 66

Visuddhi Chakra, 110

Vivekananda, Swami, 47, 61, 65–66, 101

Vyana, 110

Vyasa, 116–17, 120–21, 130

Wallace, Dr. Keith, 88

Webb, James, 31

Weed, Joseph, 91–92, 117

Weldon, John, 51, 106

Wells, H. G., 12–13

Whalen, William, 50

White, Rhen A, 92

Wilhelm, Richard, 55

Wood, Ernest, 28, 87–88

Woodroffe, Sir John, 37

World Plan Executive Council, 7

Yogananda, Paramahansa, 80

Yogatattva Upanishads, 121–22

Yule, Colonel, 24, 28, 69